Read Me First

- Descriptions in this manual are based on default settings of Samsung Galaxy Note 9.

- All information supplied in this guide is for educational purpose only and users bear the responsibility for using it.

- All information supplied in this guide was what was available as at the time of writing this guide and it may not be 100% accurate again if there is a major firmware/software update to Samsung Galaxy Note 9.

- Depending on your local network service provider or your location/region, some of the features discussed in this guide may not be available on your Samsung Galaxy Note 9.

- Although I took tremendous effort to ensure that all pieces of information provided in this guide are correct, I would welcome your suggestions if you find out that any information provided in this guide is inadequate or you find a better way of doing some of the actions mentioned in this guide. All correspondences should be sent to pharmibrahimguides@gmail.com.

About This Guide

Finally, a simplified guide on Samsung Galaxy Note 9 is here – this guide is indeed a splendid companion for this phone.

This is a very thorough, no-nonsense guide, useful for both experts and newbies. This guide contains a lot of information on Samsung Galaxy Note 9.

It is full of actionable steps, hints, notes, screenshots and suggestions. This guide is particularly useful for newbies/beginners and seniors; nevertheless, I strongly believe that even the techy guys will find some benefits reading it.

Enjoy yourself as you go through this very comprehensive guide.

PS: Please make sure you do not give the gift of Samsung Galaxy Note 9 without giving this companion guide alongside with it. This guide makes your gift a complete one.

Table of Contents

How to Use This Guide (Please Read!)

This guide is an unofficial manual of Samsung Galaxy Note 9 and it should be used just like you use any reference book or manual.

To quickly find a topic, please use the table of contents. In addition, you can use the index at the back of this book to search for keywords mentioned in this book. This would allow you to quickly find information and save time.

When I say you should carry out a set of tasks, for example, when I say you should tap **Settings > Sound > Notifications & actions**, what I mean is that you should tap on **Settings** and tap on **Sound**. And lastly, you should tap on **Notifications & actions**. Finally, when a function is enabled or turned on, the status switch will appear bold and colored. On the other hand, when a function is disabled or turned off, the status switch will appear gray.

Icons Used in This Book

I used some icons throughout this book and it is important you know what they mean.

 : I used this icon to represent **tips** and **hints**.

 : I used this icon to represent **notes**.

 : I used this icon to represent **troubleshooting tips**.

 : I used this icon when explaining a **jargon**.

I hope this guide helps you get the most out of your smartphone.

Getting Started with Your Phone

Unpacking Your Device

It is quite easy to unbox your Samsung Galaxy Note 9. Just use your hand to press the inner box so that it sticks out. Then use a knife to cut the seal (if any) and carefully open the box.

When you unpack your product box, check your product box for the following items:

1. Samsung Galaxy Note 9 with S Pen
2. USB charging cable & power adapter
3. Quick Start Guide
4. Earphones
5. Tweezers and Pen nibs
6. USB connector (USB Type-C)
7. Eject Pin (the eject pin is located on the case that house the "quick start guide")
8. Micro USB Connector
9. Rubber case (it appears not every Samsung Galaxy Note 9 comes with a rubber case).

💡 I would advise that you are careful when removing the eject pin from the case (the eject pin is located on the case that houses the "quick start guide") so as not to prick your hand in the process.

Turning Your Phone On/Off and Setting Up Your Phone

Just like many other smartphones, turning on your device is as simple as ABC. To turn on your phone, press and hold the power key until you notice a little vibration. If you are turning on your phone for the first time, please carefully follow the on-screen instructions to set it up. You will have the option to connect to a Wireless network during the setup, to learn more about connecting your phone to Wi-Fi, go to page 383. In addition, I would advise that you insert the SIM Card before switching on your phone. To learn more about inserting the SIM card, go to page 23.

To turn off your phone, press and hold the power key and select **Power off.** Select **Power off** again to confirm.

If you don't feel like switching off your phone again and you want to dismiss the power off screen, simply tap the back button. Alternatively, tap anywhere outside the onscreen icons.

In addition, if you are using the phone for the first time, remove any protective nylon from the surface of the phone.

Please do not be annoyed if you find it unnecessary reading about how to on/off your device. I have included it, in case there may be someone reading this guide who is a complete novice and knows close to nothing about smartphones.

- Some network providers may require you to enter a PIN when you switch on your phone. You can try entering **0000.** This is the default PIN for many network providers. If you have a problem entering the correct PIN, please contact your network service provider.

- During the setup, you may skip a process by tapping **SKIP** located at the bottom of the screen. Usually, you will have the option to perform this process in the future by going to the phone settings.

- While using your phone for the first time, you may have the option to transfer your contents from your old phone to Samsung Galaxy Note 9. Just carefully follow the on-screen instructions to do this. If you skip the process of content transfer during the phone setup and you will like to perform the transfer now, please see page 38 to learn how to go about this.

- Because of software updates and installations, it is likely that Samsung Galaxy Note 9 will consume a large amount of data during the setup, I would advise that you connect to a wireless network if you can. Using a mobile network during the setup might be expensive.

- When you start using Samsung Galaxy Note 9, you may probably notice that its screen locks within few seconds after you finish interacting with it. To allow the screen stay longer before it locks, change the screen timeout setting. To do this:

  o Swipe down from the top of the screen and select settings icon .
  o Tap **Display**.
  o Scroll down and tap on **Screen Timeout**. Then choose an option.

‹   **SCREEN TIMEOUT**

○   15 seconds

◉   30 seconds

○   1 minute   ⬅ **Choose an option**

○   2 minutes

○   5 minutes

○   10 minutes

Please note that selecting a longer timeout may make your battery discharge faster.

Do you need to charge your phone before first use?

To the best of my knowledge, it is not necessary. If you charge it before first use, that is cool, but if there is no way to charge it, then you can use it straightaway without charging it. I have learnt that the new lithium batteries used in smartphones don't really need to be charged before first use (provided that the battery still has power).

Get to Know Your Device

Device Layout

Number	Function
1.	LED indicator. This gives different colors depending on what is happening on the phone.
2.	Iris Detection LED

3.	Proximity/light sensors
4.	Receiver/Earpiece
5.	Front camera
6.	Iris scanner
7.	Power button
8.	Touch screen
9.	Bixby button
10.	Volume up and down button
11.	Fingerprint scanner
12.	Heart rate sensor
13.	Flash
14.	Rear camera
15.	Rear camera
16.	S Pen
17.	SIM and memory card tray
18.	S Pen/S Pen port
19.	Speaker
20.	Microphone. Please ensure you don't block the microphone while making a call.
21.	USB port and charging port (multipurpose port)
22.	Headset jack

Swiping the Screen Properly

From time to time, you would need to interact with your phone by swiping the screen with your finger. If you don't swipe it properly, you may not get the desired result. You can swipe to perform the following actions:

1. **Access the notification menu or quick settings**

To access the notification menu or quick settings, swipe down from the top of the screen. Please make sure you are starting from the top of the screen (around the earpiece/receiver area) to get the desired result. See the picture below.

If you don't start swiping from the top of the screen, you might open the applications screen instead.

2. **Accessing the app screen**

To access the applications screen, swipe up from the lower part of the screen. See the direction of the arrow below.

To go back to the home screen while on the applications screen, just swipe up or down from the middle (or around the middle) of the screen.

Get to Know Settings Tab

I think it is cool I introduce you to settings tab because I would be referring to this tab a lot.

The settings tab has many subsections and because of this, I would advise you use the

Search menu (denoted by the lens icon ⌕) to quickly find what you are looking for. To use the settings search feature, swipe down from the top of the screen and tap the settings icon (see the picture below).

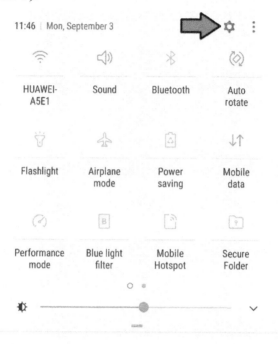

Then tap on the search icon and type a keyword corresponding to the settings you are looking for. For example, if you are looking for settings relating to battery, just type **Battery** into the search bar. The result filters as you type.

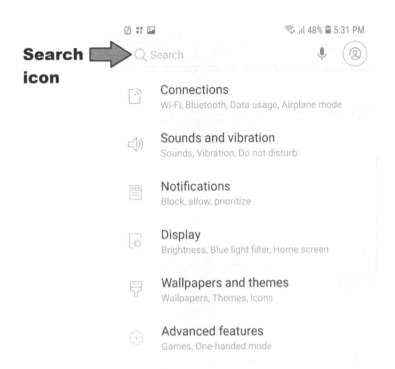

You can search the settings with your voice instead of typing. This appears cool and smart. To use this feature, just tap the microphone button and say a word or a phrase. For example, you may say **battery** if you want to search for settings relating to battery.

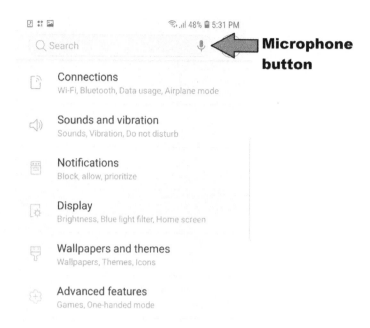

To search another phrase or word, simply tap the **X** icon next to the present word/phrase, tap the microphone button again and say a new phrase/word.

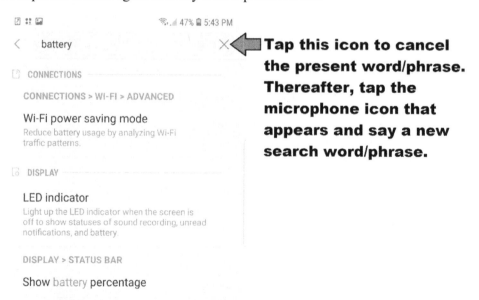

Charging Your Device

If you use your Samsung Galaxy Note 9 more often (especially if you use Wi-Fi frequently), you may realize that you need to charge your phone every day or twice a day. One of the coolest times to charge your device is when you are taking a shower, as you are not likely to be using it at the time.

Do you need to charge your phone before the first use?

Please see the answer on page 5.

To learn more on how to use your phone for a longer time on battery, please go to page 405.

To charge your Samsung Galaxy Note 9:

1. When you first open your product box, you will notice that the power cord consists of two parts (i.e. the USB cable and the USB power adapter), connect these two parts together. See the picture below.

2. Connect the end of the USB cable to the charging port of your device, making sure that both the charging cable and the charging port on your device make a good and firm contact.

3. Plug the power adapter to an electrical outlet. When your phone is charging, a charging icon will appear at the top of the screen. When your phone is fully charged, the battery icon will appear solid/full.

After charging, you may need to apply a small force to remove the USB cord from the phone. Please be careful so that the phone does not mistakenly drop from your hand in the process.

4. To know the estimated charging time remaining, swipe down from the top of the screen and tap **Settings** > **Device Maintenance** > **Battery**. The charging time may be longer if you are using your device while charging it.

- To know the detailed usage of your battery since your phone was last fully charged, go to **Settings** > **Device Maintenance** > **Battery** > **Battery Usage**.

- To extend the power of your device substantially, swipe down from the top of the screen and tap **Settings** > **Device Maintenance** > **Battery**. Under **Power saving mode** tab, tap MID or MAX and tap **APPLY**.

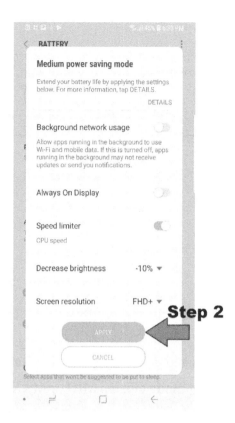

✗ Please note that if you choose MID or MAX, your phone may cause some app or functions to stop working properly in order to save battery. If you see that some apps or features are not working as they should, check if you have not enabled MID or MAX power saving mode.

- There are some apps out there that will consume your battery even without using them. Interestingly, you can prevent these apps from doing this. To do this, swipe down from the top of the screen and tap settings ⚙ > **Device Maintenance** > **Battery**. Under **App power monitor** tab, select the apps you want to prevent and tap **SAVE POWER.**

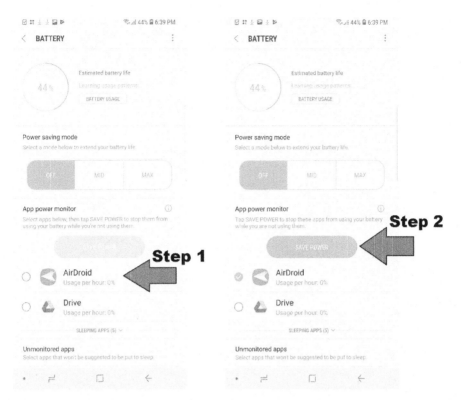

In addition, if there is an app that you want to give unrestricted battery access to, tap **Unmonitored apps** (located at the bottom of the screen) and tap **Add apps**. Select the app you want and tap **DONE** located at the top of the screen.

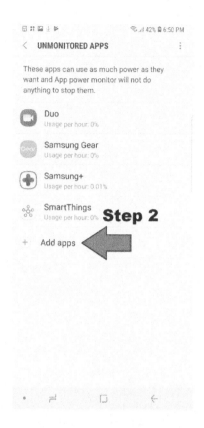

To remove an app from **Unmonitored apps** tab, swipe down from the top of the screen and tap settings ⚙ > **Device Maintenance** > **Battery** > **Unmonitored apps.** Then tap and hold the app(s) you want to delete. Tap **Delete** (located at the top of the screen) to remove the app from Unmonitored apps tab. Note that the app is not removed from your device, it is only removed from those apps that have unrestricted access to your battery.

In addition, if you do not want an app to consume your battery by running in the background, you can put it to sleep. To do this, swipe down from the top of the screen and tap settings ⚙ > **Device Maintenance** > **Battery** > **Always sleeping apps.** Then tap **Add apps**. Select the app you want and tap **DONE** located at the top of the screen.

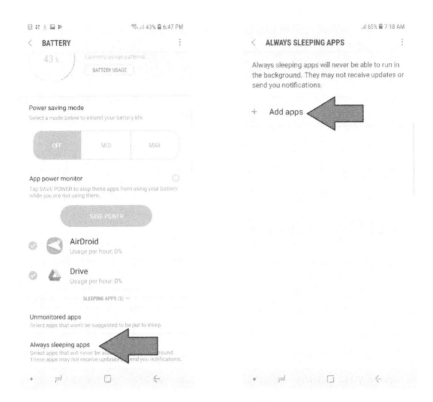

To remove an app from **Always sleeping apps** tab, tap **Always sleeping apps.** Then tap and hold the app(s) you want to delete. Tap **Delete** (located at the top of the screen). Note that the app is not removed from your device, it is only removed from those apps that are not able to run in the background.

Please note that not all app can be put to sleep using this method.

Warning: Please note that it is not advisable to use the multipurpose port while it is wet. If your phone has contact with water or any watery substance, please make sure you dry the multipurpose port before using it. Although Samsung Galaxy Note 9 is water resistant, it is not advisable at all to charge it while the device is wet. This may cause an electric shock or damage your device.

Multipurpose Jack

Using the Fast Charging Feature

Your device is built with a battery charging technology that charges the battery faster by increasing the charging power. This feature can allow you to charge the device up to 50% in about 45-55 minutes. Interestingly, Samsung Galaxy Note 9 supports fast wired charging and fast wireless charging.

Please note that using your phone while charging may affect the time your phone is going to take to make a complete charging cycle.

You can enable or disable the fast charging settings by going to Settings >

Device Maintenance > **Battery**. Then tap on menu icon located at the top of the screen. Select **Advanced Settings** > **Fast cable charging**.

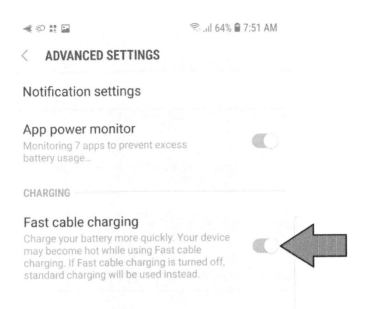

Furthermore, you might not be able to use the fast charging feature when you charge the battery using a standard battery/phone charger. To use **Fast Charging** on your device, you might need to connect it to a battery charger that supports Adaptive fast charging like the one that came with your device. To know if a battery charger supports this feature, check the charger for *Adaptive fast charging* inscription.

Although, the fast charging technology on Samsung Galaxy Note 9 is a cool feature, it may still be affected by factors like the temperature of the phone. If the device heats up for one reason or the other, the charging speed may decrease.

What About the Wireless Charging?

Samsung Galaxy Note 9 has a built-in wireless charging feature and this means that you can charge your device's battery using a wireless charger (sold separately).

To charge your device wirelessly:

- Connect the power adapter that came with your wireless charger (sold separately) to the charging port on your wireless charger. Thereafter, plug it to a wall socket.

- If you are using your wireless charger for the first time, remove any protective nylon from the surface of the wireless charger. Then, place your mobile device on the wireless charger following the instructions provided by the manufacturer of the wireless charger. Please note that if you connect a charger to your mobile device during wireless charging, the wireless charging feature might be unavailable.

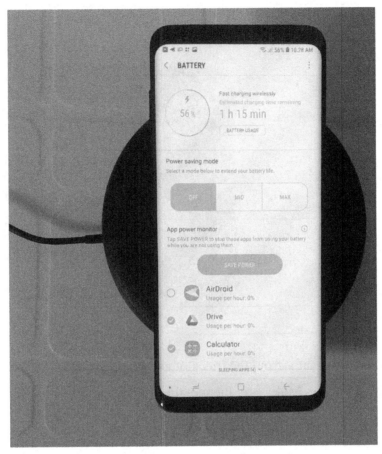

In addition, depending on the type of the wireless charger you are using, charging wirelessly may take a longer time when compared to using a cable. This means that if you want to charge your device faster, consider using a cable.

Inserting and Managing SD Card or SIM Card

Samsung Galaxy Note 9 supports the use of external memory card.

To insert memory card or SIM card:

1. Locate the SIM and SD card tray on the top edge of the device and gently insert the eject tool included with your phone into the eject hole (located at the top edge of your phone). Then push until the tray pops out. *Please note that you may need to apply a small force before the tray pops out.*

2. Pull out the tray gently from the tray slot and place the SIM card on its tray and the SD Card on its tray. Make sure the metallic contacts on the SIM and the SD card are facing down.

Please note that SIM 2 would not be available on your phone if you don't buy the dual SIM version. In addition, if you are using the dual SIM version, you may not be able to use a second SIM and the external memory card at the same time. This is because both the second SIM (SIM 2) and the external memory card use the same space.

*However, you may still be able to get a second SIM and external memory card to work simultaneously if you use a dual SIM adapter. Just search for **dual SIM adapter** on amazon.com to get started.*

After inserting the SIM and memory card, the whole setup will look like this. See the picture below.

3. Slide the card tray back into the slot.

4. Please note that if the SIM card or the memory card is not inserted properly, your phone might not recognize it. Please endeavor to follow the instructions provided above to avoid this.

5. To locate the memory card after inserting it, swipe up from the bottom of the screen and tap **Samsung** folder > **My Files**. Then tap the **SD Card** folder.

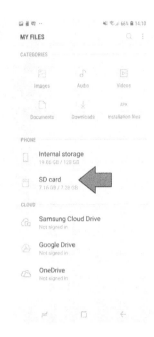

Since Samsung Galaxy Note 9 device is water resistant, you may be tempted to drop it in water at one time or the other. Please make sure that you fully insert the card tray into the tray slot before dropping the phone inside water so as to prevent liquid from entering your device.

As a rule, you must always make sure you prevent water from entering the inner compartment of the phone. Therefore, please make sure you properly close any slot you have opened on your phone before dipping it into water.

When the memory card is properly installed, you should see the memory card icon on the status bar at the top of the screen.

To remove the SD Card:

1. Swipe down from the top of the screen and select the settings icon .

2. Scroll down and tap **Device Maintenance**.

3. Tap **Storage**.

4. Tap the **menu icon** (the three dots icon located at the top of the screen).

5. Tap **Storage settings**.

6. Tap **Unmount icon** and gently open the SD card slot using the ejection pin (as you have done above). Close the SD card slot when you are done removing the memory card.

Please note that if you unmount the memory card without removing it from your device, you would need to mount it before it can be accessed again. To mount your memory card, follow the steps one to five above and tap **Unmounted**. Then select **Mount** when prompted.

Encrypt SD Card

You may wish to encrypt your memory card for extra security.

- From the Home screen, swipe up from the bottom of the screen and tap **Settings.**

- Tap **Biometrics and security**

- Scroll down and tap **Encrypt SD card**.

- Please read all the on-screen information that appears.

‹   **ENCRYPT SD CARD**

> You can encrypt SD cards. Encrypted SD cards can only be read on the device used to encrypt them. Tap ENCRYPT SD CARD to start the encryption process.
>
> Encryption could take an hour or more. Before you start, make sure that the battery is charged and keep the device plugged in until encryption is complete. During the encryption process, the SD card cannot be used. If your device is reset to factory default settings, it will be unable to read encrypted SD cards.

Read all the information above

- If you are satisfied with the information, tap **Encrypt SD card** located at the bottom of the screen and follow the on-screen instructions to encrypt all the data on your memory card.

When you encrypt your memory card, you may need a numeric PIN or password to decrypt your SD card when you first access it after switching on your device. In addition, *please note that encrypting a memory card may make it unreadable on another device.*

Formatting the memory card

1. Swipe down from the top of the screen and select the settings icon .
2. Tap **Device Maintenance**
3. Tap **Storage.**

4. Tap the **menu icon** (the three dots icon located at the top of the screen).

5. Then select **Storage settings**

6. Tap **SD card**. (Please make sure you tap the "SD card" and not the unmount icon next to it).

7. Tap **Format**, read the on-screen information and tap **Format**.

Please note that formatting a memory card will cause you to lose all the files stored on the memory card and you may need to backup your files before initiating this process.

To transfer apps from internal storage to SD Card:

Please note that many apps don't allow you to move them to the SD card. In fact, majority of the apps I have tested can't be moved to the SD Card.

1. Swipe down from the top of the screen and tap **Settings** .
2. Tap **Apps**.
3. Tap the app you want to transfer.
4. Select **Storage** from the options that appear.
5. Next to the name of the app you want to transfer, tap **Change**.

6. Tap **SD card.**

7. Tap **Move** located at bottom of the screen and wait for the process to finish.

You may consider removing temporary files from your device to free up space. From the Home screen, swipe up from the bottom of the screen and tap **Settings** ⚙ > **Device Maintenance**. Tap **Storage** and tap **Clean Now**.

Please note that using this method may clear cached data for all apps. Cache data can loosely be defined as temporary files from an application or website stored on your device to ease your interaction with the application or website.

If your phone is hanging or misbehaving, consider cleaning the memory. To do this,

from the Home screen, swipe up from the bottom of the screen and tap **Settings** >
Device Maintenance. Tap **Memory** and tap **Clean Now.**

Maintaining the Water and Dust Resistance

Although your Samsung Galaxy Note 9 is water and dust resistant, there are few things you still have to put at the back of your mind so that you don't damage your phone. Some of the things you have to know are discussed below:

- Even though your device is water resistant, you can't still immerse the device in water deeper than 1.5 m and/or keep it submerged for more than 30 minutes.
- The water you want to put your phone inside should be a fresh water and it should have temperature between 15 - 35°C and pressure between 86 and 106 kPa.
- The screen of your device may not respond properly while under water or wet. I will advice that you clean it with a dry towel to get the full functionality.

- It is not advisable to put your device under water moving with force such as tap water. This is because water may get into the inner part of your device in the process.

- While the phone's screen is wet, you may not enjoy the optimal function of your device as you should. You may need to clean it with a dry towel to make it work properly.

- To avoid electric shock, please don't charge your device while it is wet or under water.

- If your phone falls from a considerable height, it may affect its water resistivity.

- Avoid putting your phone in a liquid other than water. In addition, avoid putting your phone inside salt water or ionized water.

Samsung Galaxy Note 9 may not respond to touch while under water but it should respond to touch immediately you take it out of water. But don't forget that you can't drop it inside water while the SIM/memory slot is opened. In addition, please don't charge your phone while it is wet to avoid electric shock.

Moving Your Items from Your Old Phone to Your Galaxy Note 9

You can move your files to your new phone by following the steps mentioned below:

- The easiest way to transfer your items from your old phone (Android Phone or IOS Phone) to your new Samsung Galaxy Note 9 is by using a USB connector (On-the-Go (OTG) connector) and a USB cable. To use this method, please follow the instructions below:

  Please make sure you download and install Smart Switch app on your old phone before you begin the transfer process. Smart Switch can be downloaded from Google Play Store. In addition, this method of data transfer consumes a large amount of energy, make sure your phone is fully charged before initiating this process.

  To transfer content via cable:

  - Plug the USB connector (On-the-Go (OTG) connector) that came with your device into the multipurpose jack of your device.

- Then connect your device and the old phone using a USB cable. Please note that you are to select Media device (MTP) option on your old phone if prompted. The whole connection would look like this (see below). *Please note that you may need to download, install and open Samsung Smart Switch Mobile on your old phone to complete this process.* **Samsung Smart Switch Mobile** app can be downloaded from Google Play Store.

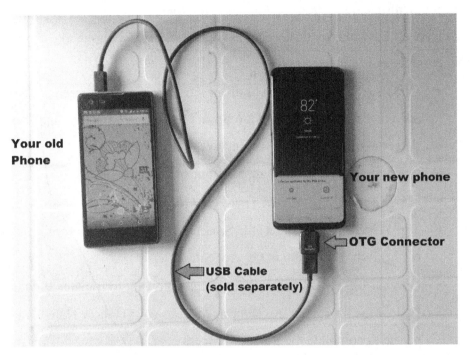

- When prompted, tap **Smart Switch** and select **Just Once**. If you are not prompted, disconnect the cable, then reconnect.

- Tap **Start**.

- Tap **Agree** if you agree with the terms/condition.

- Read the onscreen information and tap **OK** if you agree with the information.

- On the old phone open **Samsung Smart Switch Mobile** app and follow the prompts.

- Tap **Receive** on your Samsung Galaxy Note 9.

- Your device will recognize the old phone and a list of data you can transfer will appear. Select what you want to transfer and tap **Transfer.**

- Follow the on-screen instructions to complete the data transfer process.
- Alternatively, if the USB connector and the USB cable are not accessible, you can send items from your old phone to your new phone wirelessly using Smart Switch app. Please note that you will need to download and install **Samsung Smart Switch Mobile** app on your old phone to complete this process. In addition, you would need to switch on the Wi-Fi on your new and old phone to use this option.

  To transfer content wirelessly:

  - On Galaxy Note 9, swipe up from the bottom of the screen to access app screen. Tap **Samsung** and tap **Smart Switch**. Thereafter, tap **Start > Agree > OK > Wireless > Receive > Android**.
  - Open the **Smart Switch** app on your old phone.
  - Tap **Start** and tap **Agree**. Then, tap **OK**.
  - Tap **Wireless.** Thereafter, the Smart Switch app should try to establish connection. If prompted, tap **Accept.**
  - On your old phone, select those items you want to transfer and tap **Send**.
  - Follow the on-screen instructions on both your Galaxy Note 9 and the old phone to complete the transfer process.
  - When the transfer process is complete, tap **Close App**.
- I would like to mention that you can also transfer items from your old phone to your new device using a memory card. All you have to do is to insert a memory card into your old phone, transfer your content to the memory card, remove the memory card and place it inside your Samsung Galaxy Note 9.
- Lastly, you can transfer your items from your old phone to your new phone by using cloud storage. For example, you can use OneDrive App. To do this, add files to OneDrive app on your old phone so that you can access them from your Samsung Galaxy Note 9. To move a file to OneDrive, simply upload it using the plus + icon located in the OneDrive app or send the files to your OneDrive folder. Once the files are on OneDrive, you can access them on your Samsung Galaxy Note 9 by opening the OneDrive app. To avoid any problem while trying to access

your files, please ensure that you are connected to a browsing network while trying to access OneDrive.

Please note that you may need to download OneDrive app to your phones to use this method.

Using the Touch Screen

Your phone's touch screen allows you to easily select items and perform functions. With the touch screen, you may operate your phone like a pro.

Notes:

- Do not press the touch screen with your fingertips, or use sharp tools on the touch screen. Doing so may cause malfunctioning.

- Do not allow the touch screen to come into contact with other electrical appliances. This may cause the touch screen to malfunction.

- When the touch screen is wet, endeavor to clean it with a dry towel before using it. The touchscreen may not function properly when wet.

- For optimal use of the screen, you may need to remove screen protector before using it. However, a good screen protector should be usable with your phone.

You may control your touch screen with the following actions:

Tap: Touch once with your finger to select or launch a menu, application or option.

Tap and hold: Tap an item and hold it for a second to open a list of options.

Tap and drag: Tap and drag with your finger, to move an item to a different location in the application grid/list.

Pinch: Place two fingers far apart, then draw them closer.

💡 If you are using a screen protector, you may consider increasing the touch sensitivity of your phone for optimum usage. To do this, swipe up from the bottom of the screen and tap **Settings** 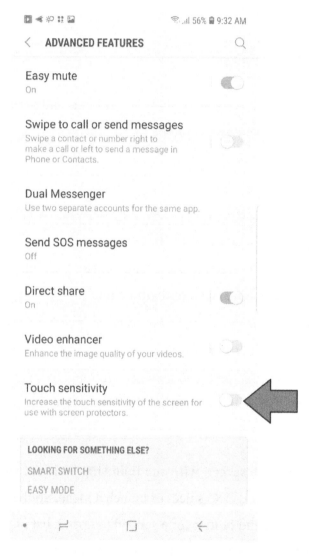 > **Advanced Features** > **Touch sensitivity.** Then tap the indicator switch next to **Touch sensitivity**.

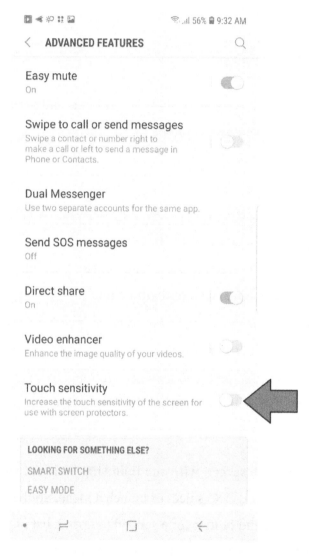

💡 You can control the screen with just one hand when you enable one-handed mode. To enable this mode:

1. Swipe down from the top of the screen and tap settings icon .

2. Tap **Advanced features**.

3. Tap **One-handed Mode**.

If you realized that your phone accidentally detects touches when you don't want, for example when the phone is inside your pocket, you could block accidental touches. To do this, go to **Settings** > **Display** > **Block accidental touches**.

To Lock or Unlock the touch screen

When you do not use the device for a specified period, your device turns off the touch screen and automatically locks so as to prevent any unwanted device operations and save battery. To manually lock the touch screen, press the power key.

To unlock, turn on the screen by pressing the power key (or double tap the home button

) and swipe up in any direction. If you have already set a lock screen password, you will be prompted to enter the password instead of swiping.

You can change the lock screen method on your phone, please refer to page 126 to learn how to do this.

Rotating the touch screen

Your phone has a built-in motion sensor that detects its orientation. If you rotate the device, the screen should automatically rotate according to the orientation.

➢ **To activate or deactivate screen rotation**

To quickly disable or enable screen rotation, swipe down from the top of the screen and tap . Please note that when the screen rotation icon appears gray, the screen rotation is disabled.

Using the Dedicated Back Button

You may use the dedicated back button (see the picture below) to view the previous page or go back to a previous menu. Back button can also be used to close a dialog box, menu, or keyboard.

In addition, you may use the dedicated back button on your device to get out of any page when you are done with the page and you don't see the "done" option.

Back button is one of the components of navigation bar. To learn how to manage navigation bar like a pro, see page 87.

Using the In-APP Back Button

There are some apps that give you the opportunity to go back to the previous screen using

the in-app back button   <   . When available, this button can be found at the upper left part of the screen.

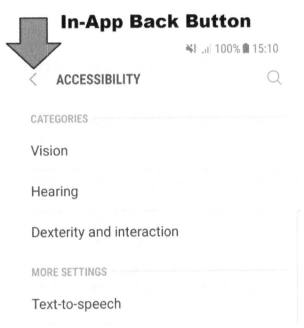

Getting to Know the Menu icon

The menu icon is the three dots icon ⋮ that usually appears at the top of the screen when you open an app. This icon can also be called **hidden options icon**. This is because it contains more options about an app or item.

Your phone's maintenance status is excellent.
Tap below to improve it.

Whenever you are thinking of accessing more options when using an app/item or you are thinking of using an app in a new way, just tap on the menu icon.

Getting to Know the Home Screen

From your Home screen, you can view your phone's status and access applications. Scroll left or right to see different apps on the Home screen. Please note that the Home screen usually has many screens and you can add more screens by tapping on +. More on this shortly.

Home Screen Layout

Number	Function
1.	**Status icons**: These icons tell you more about your device. For example, if the Wi-Fi is turned on, you would see the Wi-Fi status icon on the top right part of the screen.
2.	**Edge Handle**: Swipe left on this handle to display edge icons.
3.	**Home Screen Indicator:** This indicates which home screen is currently visible

4.	**Back Button**.
5.	**Home Button**
6.	**Recent App button**
7.	**App shortcuts**: Tap any of these icons to launch the corresponding app.
8.	**Notification icon**: When you see a notification icon appearing at the top left part of the screen, simply swipe down from the top of the screen to learn more about this notification icon or see the notification detail.

Customizing the Home Screen

To get more out of the Home screen, you would need to perform some tweaks. To customize the Home screen to your taste:

1. While on the Home screen, place your two fingers on the screen and move them closer or tap and hold an empty space on the Home screen. To go to the Home screen from any screen, press the Home button .

Empty Space

2. Then you will see a screen that looks like the one below.

3. You can perform any of the following actions:

    o   **Add a screen**: To do this, swipe left until you see the plus/Add **(+)** icon. Tap this icon to add a new screen.

In addition, you can add app icons to a Home screen. To do this, tap and hold an app icon on the applications screen, then select **Add to Home**.

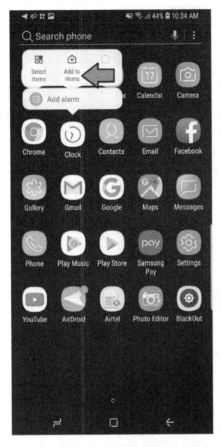

To move an app icon from one Home screen to another, tap, hold and drag the app icon to the edge of the screen and wait for the screen to turn. Do this until you get to the desired screen, then lift your finger.

Tap and hold the app icon you want to move, then move it to the right edge or left edge of the screen until the page turns. When the app icon is in right position, lift your finger.

○ **Remove a screen**: To do this, swipe left until you see the Home screen you want to remove. Then tap the **Delete** icon located on top of the screen that you want to delete.

Delete icon

Wallpapers   Themes   Widgets   Home screen settings

o **Change the order of the Home screens:** To do this, tap and hold a screen and drag it to the edge of the screen until the page turns. When the Home screen is in the right position, lift your finger.

Tap and hold the screen you want to move, then move it to the right edge or left edge of the screen until the page turns. When the screen is in the right position, lift your finger.

To easily access a Home screen, you may consider setting it as your **main** Home screen. Please see below.

○ **Set a screen as the main Home screen:** To do this, swipe left or right until the screen is visible, then tap the **Home button** located at the top of the screen. When a screen is your main Home screen, the Home screen button appears bold.

To access the Home screen at any point in time, press the dedicated

Home button .

- ○ **Bixby Home**: To access Bixby Home, swipe right. To enable or disable this feature, tap the status switch. To learn more about Bixby, go to page 194.

To move out of a setting when you are done, tap the back button.

Back button

Do you want to increase or decrease the number of apps that appear in a row on the Home screen? If yes, go to page 69 to learn more.

Add/Remove an app shortcut to the Home screen

You can add apps/items to the Home screen so that you can easily access them anytime.

To do this:

1. Access the app screen by swiping up the screen while on the Home screen.
2. While in the app screen, tap and hold an app icon and select **Add to Home**.

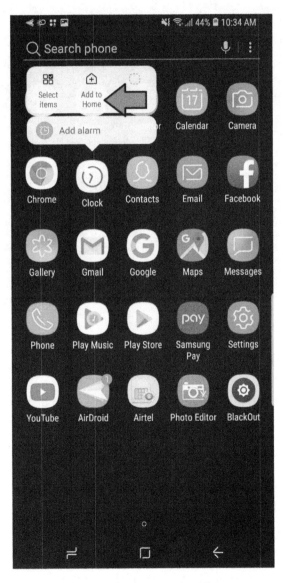

3. To move an app icon to a new location on the Home screen, simply tap, hold and drag it to that location.

4. To remove an app icon from the Home screen, tap and hold the app icon you want to remove, then select **Remove from Home**. Please note that removing an app icon from the home screen does not uninstall the app, it merely removes it from the Home screen.

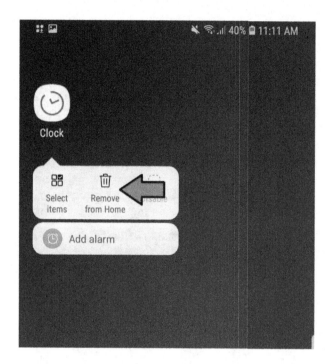

Managing the Home screen widget

A widget is a small item that allows you to control an app in a special way. Widgets display information and invite users to act in special ways.

To add a widget to a Home screen:

1. While on the Home screen, place two fingers on the screen, then move them closer, or tap and hold an empty space on the Home screen. To go to the Home screen from any screen, press the Home button ⬜ .

2. Tap on **Widgets** located at the bottom of the screen.

3. Swipe left or right to see the available widgets, then tap a category. Tap and hold a widget from the list of the widgets that appear, drag it to a Home screen and release it.

4. To move a widget to a new location, tap, hold and drag the widget to the desired location. Tap outside the widget to save the changes.

5. To remove a widget from a Home screen, tap and hold the widget, then select **Remove from Home screen**.

6. To resize a resizable widget, touch and hold, then release the widget. Thereafter, drag the rectangular blue outline to your desired size. Tap outside of the widget to save the changes. *Please note that you may not be able to resize all widgets.*

Rectangular Outline

In addition, please note that you may not be able to adjust the size of some widgets vertically.

Managing the Home screen theme

1. While on the Home screen, place two fingers on the screen and move them closer. Alternatively, tap and hold an empty space on the home screen.
2. Tap **Theme** located at the lower side of the screen and tap **Start.** If prompted, tap **Allow**, if you agree to the request.
3. Choose a theme. *Please note that you may need to agree to Terms and Conditions before you can access themes.*

4. To search for themes, tap the search button $\mathcal{Q}$ located at the top of the screen.

Type a search phrase and hit the search icon $\mathcal{Q}$ on the virtual keyboard.

5. To see free themes, tap **VIEW ALL.**

6. When you have seen the theme you like, tap the theme and tap **Download**.

7. Wait for the theme to finish downloading and tap **Apply** (See below).

Step 6   Step 7

8. To change the theme to the default one, open themes as described in steps 1 and 2 above. Then tap the default theme and tap **Apply**.

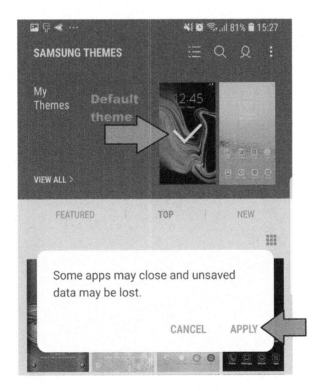

Please note that visual elements such as colors, icons, and wallpapers, may change depending on the selected theme.

Managing the Home screen wallpaper

This option allows you to change the wallpaper settings for the Home screen and the locked screen.

1. While on the Home screen, place two fingers on the screen, then move them closer. Alternatively, tap and hold an empty space on the home screen. To go to the home screen from any screen, press the home button .
2. Tap on **Wallpapers** located at the bottom of the screen.
3. To search for wallpapers, tap the search button located at the top of the screen. Type a search phrase and hit the search icon on the virtual keyboard.
4. To view free wallpapers, scroll down and tap **VIEW ALL**.

5. When you have seen the wallpaper you like, tap **Download**, then tap **Apply**.

6. Choose whether you want the wallpaper to appear on the **Home screen, Lock screen, or Home and lock screens**.

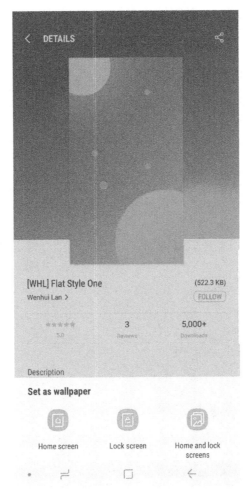

7. Select **Motion Effect**, if you want to give your wallpaper a motion effect.

Please note that "motion effect" may not be available if you choose "Lock screen" in step 6 above.

8. Tap **Set as Wallpaper.**

Please note that you might be prompted while trying to apply a wallpaper, just read the information shown to you and agree if you like.

What about the screen grid?

The screen grid option allows you to choose the number of app icons that is displayed in a row on your Home screen.

1. While on the Home screen, place two fingers on the screen, then move them closer. Alternatively, tap and hold an empty space on the home screen.
2. Tap **Home screen settings**.
3. Tap **Home screen grid**.

4. Choose a dimension. 4x5 means there are four apps in a row and five apps in a column; 4x6 means there are four apps in a row and six apps in a column; 5x5 means there are five apps in a row and five apps in a column; and 5x6 means there are five apps in a row and six apps in a column.

5. When you are done picking a dimension, tap **Apply** (located at the top of the screen).

💡 In addition, you can change the app screen grid by following a similar method. Simply repeat steps 1 and 2 above and tap Apps screen grid. Thereafter, choose an option and tap **Apply** to save the changes.

Creating a folder of items/apps on the Home Screen

1. From the Home screen or applications screen, tap and hold an app, then drag and drop it onto another item/app's icon to create a folder.

2. Tap **Enter folder name** and enter a name.

3. To change the color of the folder, tap the color icon and select a color.

4. To add another app, tap **ADD APPS** located at the bottom of the screen.

5. When you are done customizing a folder, tap the **Done** button on the virtual keyboard or tap the back icon ← or both.

6. To remove an app from a folder, tap the folder, then long-tap the app you want to remove and drag it out of the folder.
   Please note that the folder is automatically deleted when it remains only one app in the folder.

Accessing and Managing Applications

To open an app:

1. From the Home screen; swipe up from the bottom of the screen to access applications screen.

2. Tap the app of your choice.

3. To go back to the app grid screen, press the back button

Accessing Recently Opened or Running Applications

1. Tap on the recent button to show the recent apps window. This contains the list of all opened/running apps.

2. Tap an app to launch it or tap the **X** icon to close it. To close all opened apps, tap **CLOSE ALL** located at the bottom of the screen.

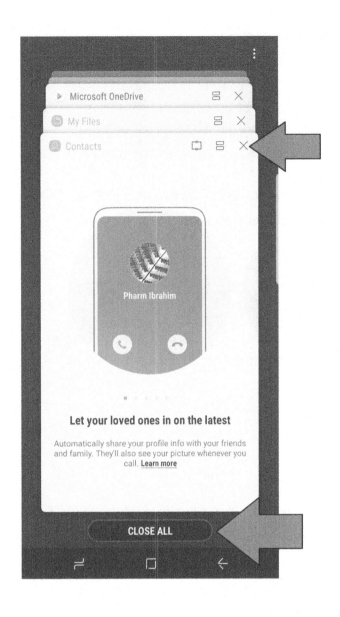

You can lock an app so that it does not get closed when you tap **CLOSE ALL.** To do

this, tap the recent button ⌐⌐ and select the menu icon ⋮ located at the top of the

screen. Then select **Lock apps.**

Tap the padlock icon next to the app you want to lock and select **DONE.** When the padlock icon is closed, then the app is locked.

Please note that although a locked app is not closed when you tap CLOSE ALL, you can still close it by swiping it to the right or left.

Advice: Although Samsung Galaxy Note 9 can run many apps at a time, multitasking may cause memory problems, or additional power consumption. To avoid these, end all unused programs by closing the app.

Uninstalling/Deleting an App

If you don't need an app again, you can uninstall it. To do this:

1. From the applications screen, locate the app you want to uninstall. Tap and hold this app, then select **Uninstall.**

2. Tap **OK** to confirm.

✖ Please note that you might not be able to uninstall apps that come preloaded on your Note 9, you might only be able to disable them. To disable an app that comes preloaded on your phone, repeat step 1 above and select **Disable**. A disabled app will be removed from the application list and will not be able to perform any action on your phone. To reenable an app, go to **Settings** > **Apps**. Then tap the app you want to enable and select **Enable**.

Managing the applications screen

Selecting Apps

You can select many apps to perform an action on all of them at the same time. To do this:

1. Tap and hold an app and tap **Select items**.

2. Then select all apps you want and choose an option at the top of the screen. If an option appears gray that means you can't use the option. For example, if your selection contains a folder, the **Create folder** icon would appear gray because you can't put a folder inside another folder. Also, you can tap and hold an app in your selection to move them to another part of the screen. In addition, you can drag the selected apps up the screen to add them to the home screen.

Usually, when there is an app notification, a badge appears on the corresponding app icon. If an app has a badge, you can clear this badge by following the method below.

- Swipe down from the top of the screen to access the notifications screen.

- Dismiss the corresponding notification on the notification screen to clear the badge. For example, if AirDroid app has a badge, you would dismiss this badge when you dismiss its notification on the notification screen. You can dismiss a notification by swiping the notification towards right or left.

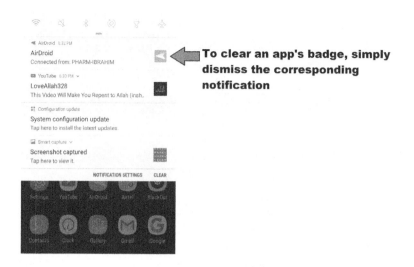

To clear an app's badge, simply dismiss the corresponding notification

Please note that a badge is a notification number displayed on an app icon, e.g.

To customize *app icon badges* settings, swipe down from the top of the screen and

tap settings icon ⚙. Type in **app icon badges** into the search bar located at the top of the screen. The result filters as you type. Tap **app icon badges** from the results that appear.

Showing the Apps Button

You can choose to show the apps button on the Home screen. To do this:

1. While on the Home screen, swipe up the screen to access the applications screen.

2. Tap the menu icon ⋮ and select **Home screen settings**.

3. Tap **Apps button** and choose **Show Apps button.** Then tap **APPLY** located at the top of the screen.

Arranging Applications Alphabetically

1. While on the Home screen, swipe up the screen to access the application screen.

2. Tap the menu icon ⋮ next to the search bar.

3. Tap **Sort** and choose an option.

📌 If you choose to arrange your apps/folders alphabetically, the folders would appear first.

Hiding Applications

If you don't want your kids to access sensitive apps on your phone, you can hide them. For example, if you don't want your children to access your shopping app, you can hide it. However, please note that people may still be able to see your hidden apps if they are tech savvy and they know the way.

To hide apps:
1. While on home screen, swipe up the screen to access the applications screen.

2. Tap the menu icon ⋮ and select **Home screen settings**.
3. Tap **Hide apps.** Then select the apps you want to hide and tap **APPLY** located at the top of the screen.

4. To unhide the apps, just repeat the steps 1 to 3 above and unselect the apps you have selected before. Then tap **APPLY** located at the top of the screen.

Managing Applications

You can force-stop a misbehaving app. In addition, you can clear cache/data to clear errors in an app or to save phone memory.

To force-stop an app and manage app settings:

1. Swipe down from the top of the screen and tap settings icon ⚙.
2. Scroll down and tap **Apps**.
3. Tap the app you want to manage.

4. To force-stop an app, tap **FORCE STOP.** Force-stopping an app is useful when an app is misbehaving or when it refuses to close. To access a force-stopped app again, just relaunch the app from the application screen.

5. To clear the cache or data of an app, tap **Storage**, then tap **CLEAR DATA** or **CLEAR CACHE.** *Please note that clearing data may cause you to lose settings, files and all other stored information on the app. Only clear the data of an app if you want to start using it as a new app.*

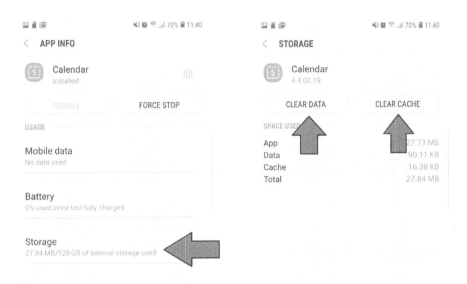

If you don't see **Clear Data** in step 5 above, then choose **Manage Storage.** When you choose **Manage Storage** option, you should be able to access Clear Data tab.

6. To manage the notification of an app, tap **Notifications** and choose an option.

7. To manage the permissions you have given to an app, scroll down and tap **Permissions**. Then choose an option.

If an app is disturbing you with notifications and you want to quickly manage notification settings, just swipe down from the top of the screen and tap **NOTIFICATION SETTINGS.** Then use the status switch next to each app to manage their notifications. To learn more about phone notifications, see page 90.

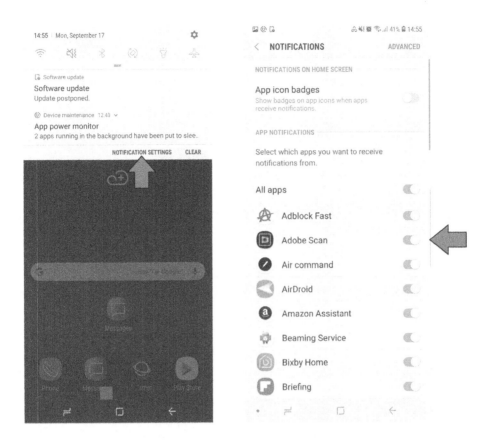

Are there any confidential documents, files or items you want to make private so that only you can access them? If yes, do the following to protect them:

Swipe down from the top of the screen and tap **Settings** 🔧 > **Biometrics and security** > **Secure folder**. Follow the on-screen instructions to complete the process.

Managing the Navigation Bar

The navigation bar is the bar at the bottom of your device screen. This bar comprises back icon, Home icon and recent apps icon. Interestingly, you can hide or unhide this bar. To manage notification bar:

1. Swipe down from the top of the screen and tap settings icon .

2. Then tap on the search icon.

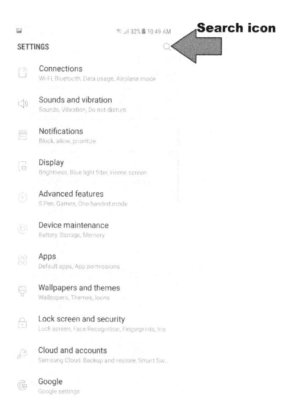

3. Type in **Navigation bar** into the search bar. The result filters as you type. Tap **Navigation bar** from the results that appear.

4. Choose an option from the Navigation bar settings screen.

5. To enable the Show and hide button, tap **Show and hide button.** Then tap the status switch next to **OFF**.

6. When this is enabled you should be able to quickly hide or show the navigation bar by double tapping the small dot icon.

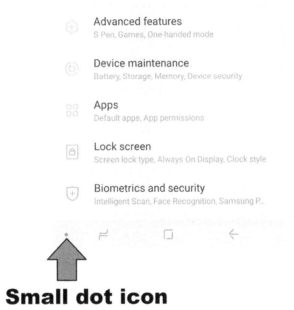

Small dot icon

7. You could also select those apps in which "show and hide button" would not appear. To do this, simply tap the status switch next to an app.

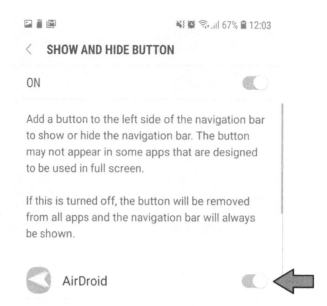

To show the navigation bar after hiding it, swipe in from the bottom of the screen. You could also use the Home button even when it is not visible. To do this simply hard press (i.e. tap with force) the area where home button normally appears. Usually, you would hear a small vibration when you press the correct spot.

Managing Phone Notifications

Notifications consume battery and it may be a source of disturbance occasionally. To manage notifications:

1. Swipe down from the top of the screen and tap settings icon ⚙ .
2. Then tap **Notifications**.
3. Use the status switch to manage notification for an individual app. To disable all notifications, tap the status switch next to **All apps** (located at the top of the screen.) To have an advanced management of notifications, tap **ADVANCED** and choose an app. You can use the advanced settings to manage apps that can give you notifications while Do Not Disturb (see page 351) is active.

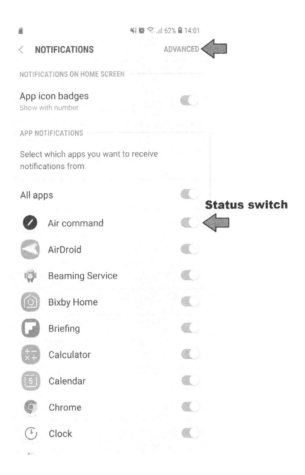

To manage notification sound on your phone, swipe down from the top of the screen

and tap **Settings** ⚙ > **Sounds and vibration** > **Notification sounds**. If using a dual SIM model, select a SIM. Then select **Silent** if you don't want a notification sound. To change your selection, choose a notification sound.

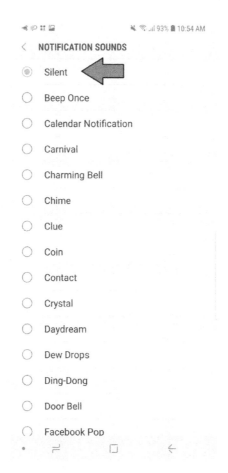

In addition, you can select whether you will see notification details or notification icon only on Home screen. To do this, swipe down from the top of the screen and tap settings icon 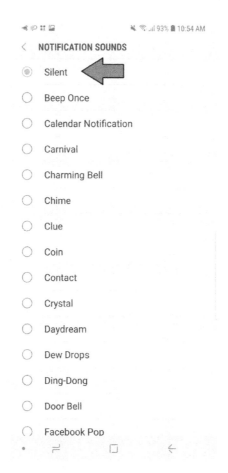, type in **app icon badges** into the search bar located at the top of the screen. The result filters as you type. Tap **app icon badges** from the results that appear. Then scroll down and tap the status switch next to **Show notifications**, (see the picture below).

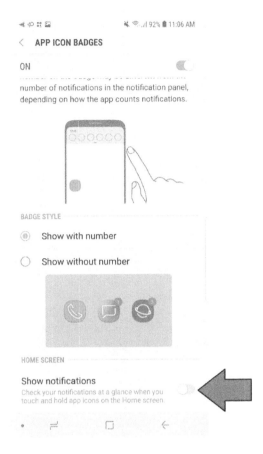

When you enable this option, you should be able to see your notifications at a glance when you touch and hold an app icon on the Home screen.

If you don't want to see any form of notification icons/badges or details on your apps screen, tap the status switch next to **ON**.

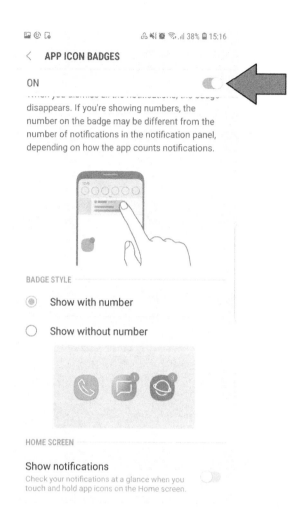

Furthermore, you can quickly block a notification from the quick action menu. To do this, simply swipe down from the top of the screen, tap and hold a notification. Then tap the status switch to block notifications from the app in question. Thereafter, tap **Save** to register the changes. To view the detailed settings of a notification, select **DETAILS**.

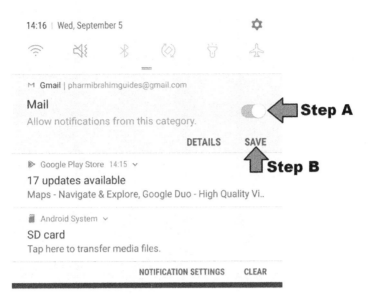

To re-enable the notification you have previously blocked, go to **Settings**, then **Apps**. Tap the app involved and tap **Notifications**. Then re-enable any deactivated option.

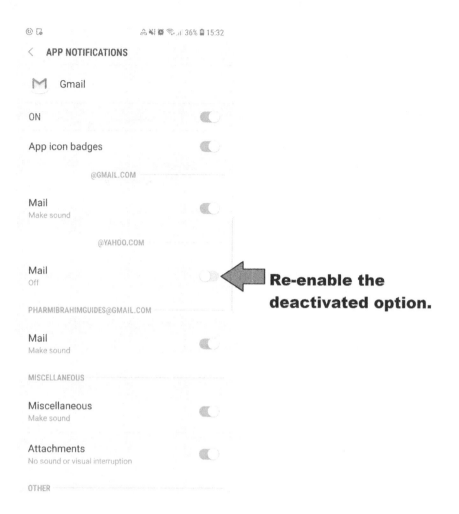

Re-enable the deactivated option.

If you are not getting notification from an app (for example, if you are not getting notifications from Email app), these are the things to check:

1. Check whether you have not blocked notifications from this app. You can know this by following the steps on page 90.

2. Confirm that you have not disabled **Sync** function. To do this, swipe down from the top of the screen with two fingers. Then swipe left and see if **Sync** appears bold. If it appears bold, then it is enabled. Please note that if *Sync* is disabled you may not get some notifications.

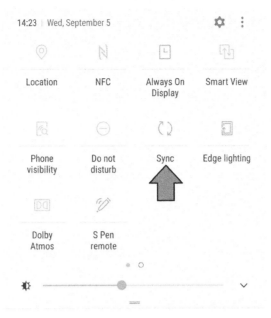

3. If the first two steps above do not work, then make sure your phone is not restricting the app's battery usage. Restricting the battery usage for an app may affect the ability of the app to get sync or use data. To know if an app has a restricted battery usage, go to **Settings** ⚙ > **Apps** > **menu icon** ⋮ (located at the top of the screen) > **Special access** > **Optimize battery usage**. Tap the dropdown menu and select **All apps**. Locate the app in question and make sure the indicator switch next to it is turned off.

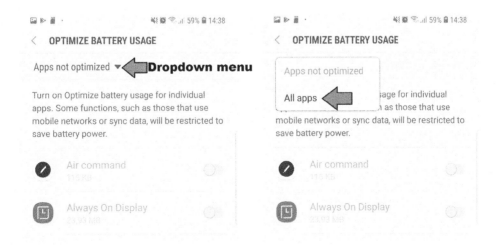

Using the Multi Window/Split-Screen Function

Multi window is one of the coolest features of Samsung Galaxy Note 9. Multi window allows you to put two apps side by side. *However, it is important to note that not all apps support multi window feature.*

Using Multi Window feature:

Before you start using multi-window/split-screen, I would advise that you enable *Use Recents button* feature. To do this:

1. Swipe down from the top of the screen and tap settings icon .
2. Tap **Advanced features**.
3. Scroll down and tap **Multi window**.

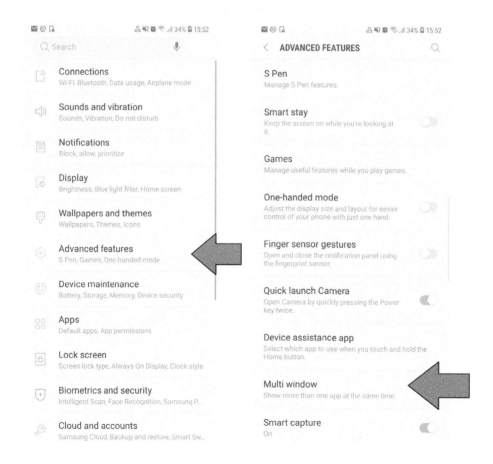

4. Tap the status switch next to **Use Recents button**.

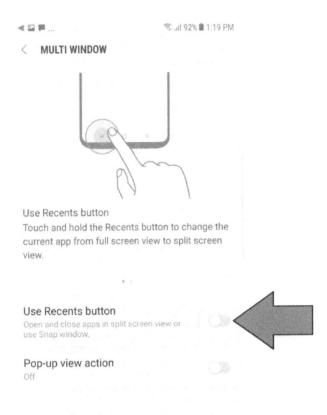

Note that when this option is enabled, you would be able to change the current app from full screen view to split-screen view by pressing and holding Recent button .

To use multi window feature:

1. Open an app that supports multi-screen (e.g. phone app).

2. Touch and hold the recent button 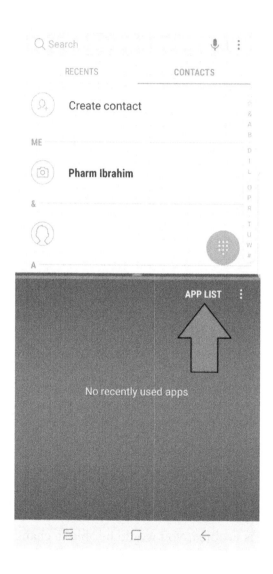, then tap **APPS LIST.**

3. Choose an app from the list that appears.

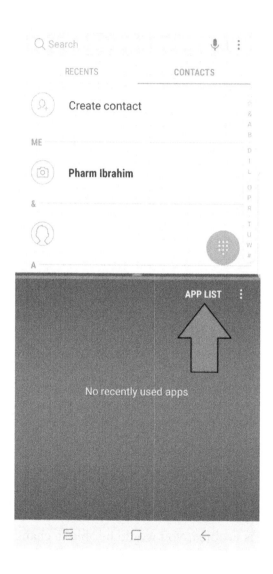

4. Alternatively, tap the recent button 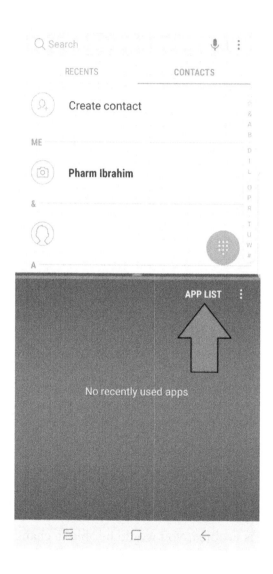 to open the list of recently used apps.

Then tap the split-screen icon 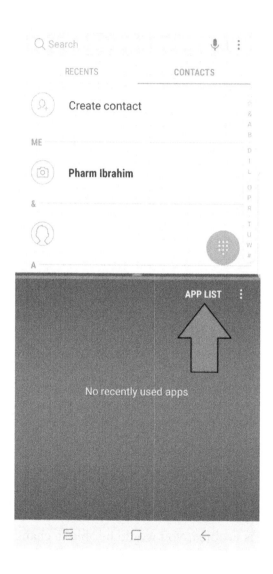 on the app you want to split. The app will launch in the upper window and the other recently used apps that support multi window will display below the launched app. Swipe up or down (if necessary) and select the second app.

5. To adjust the size of an app window, tap the middle of the dividing line between the app windows (i.e. the straight line that appears between the two app windows) and drag it up or down. See the picture below.

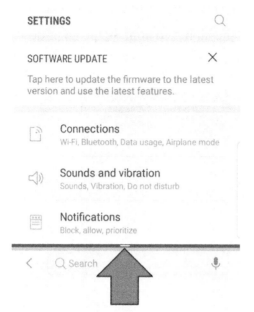

Adjust the window by dragging this small white icon

No recent searches

6. To close an app opened in split-screen, tap the split-screen icon and tap the **X** icon next to the app you want to close. See below.

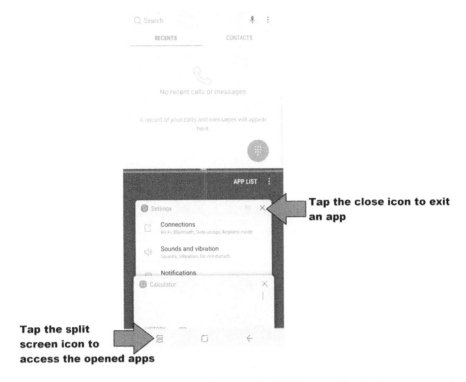

Tap the close icon to exit an app

Tap the split screen icon to access the opened apps

If you can't see the **X** icon, then the app may be locked. To unlock the app, tap the padlock icon.

Padlock icon

7. To open another app in split-screen, tap the split-screen icon [icon], tap **APP LIST** and select an app.

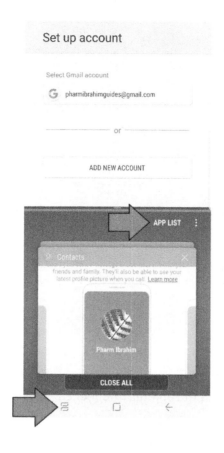

8. To exit multi window view, tap and hold the split-screen icon 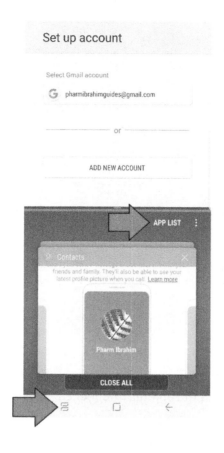 (located at the bottom of the screen).

Using the Multi Window Controls

When using apps in the split screen view, tap the middle of the dividing line between the app windows to access multi window options.

Tap this

To dismiss the multi window screen controls, tap the back button ←.

The Multi Window Options

1 2 3 4 5

Icon	Function
1.	Tap this button to add the current app pair (i.e. the current two apps you are viewing) to the home screen. This will allow you to quickly access the two apps in the future.
2.	Tap this icon to move an app window to another part (usually the top part of the screen). When you tap this icon, a blue outline will appear. Adjust this blue outline as you wish to resize the window. When you are done resizing, tap **DONE** to effect the changes.
3.	Tap this icon to switch window positions i.e. move a lower app window to upper part of the screen and vice versa.
4.	Tap this to open an app in a pop-up windows or minimize an app.
5.	Tap this icon to close the currently active app and exit the multi windows screen.

Using the Minimize icon:

1. When using apps in the split-screen view, tap the middle of the dividing line between the app windows to access multi window options.

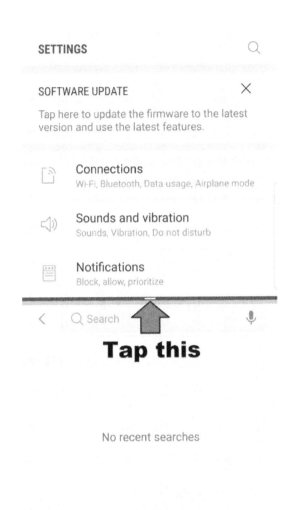

Tap this

2. Tap the minimize icon 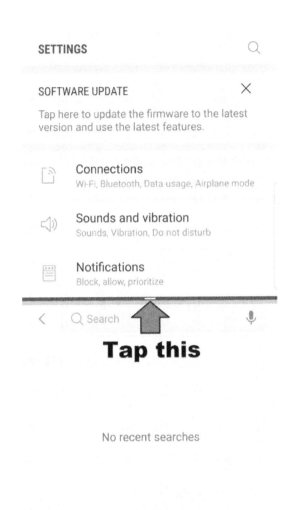 to minimize the currently active app; then tap and hold the upper part of the window next to the outline to drag the window from one part of the screen to another. To resize it however, tap, hold and move the outline as you wish.

Tap, hold and drag the upper part of the window (next to the outline) to move it to another part of the screen

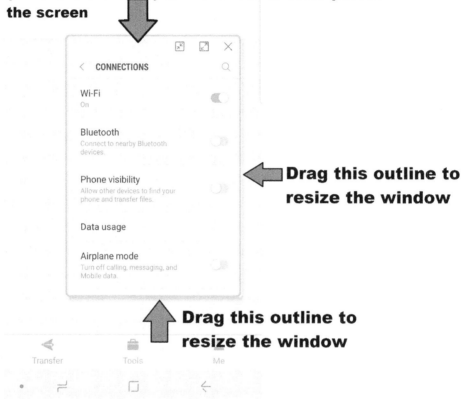

Drag this outline to resize the window

Drag this outline to resize the window

3. Tap to minimize the app window to a small icon. This small icon can be dragged from one part of the screen to another when you tap, hold and move it.

4. To maximize the window to a full screen, tap the corresponding small icon, then

   tap ⬈ . For example, if the app in question is settings app, tap the small icon

   ⚙ representing the settings app, then tap the maximize button ⬈ .

Understanding the Quick Settings menu

The Quick settings panel provides a quick access to device functions such as Wi-Fi, allowing you to quickly turn them on or off. You access Quick settings panel when you swipe down from the top of the screen.

💡 The app icon that is currently active in Quick settings menu will appear bold, so if you want to know whether you have enabled a feature or not, just check its boldness. For example, if you want to know if Bluetooth is on, swipe down from the top of the screen and see if the Bluetooth icon appears bold.

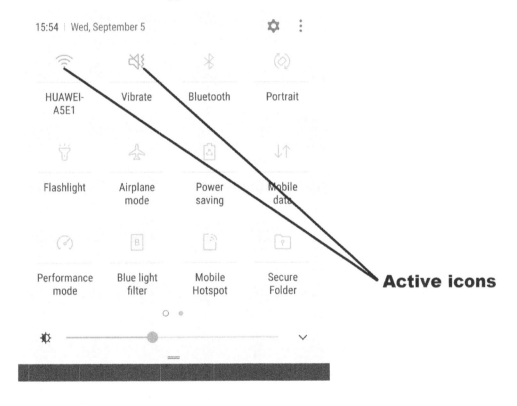

To view additional Quick settings:

1. Swipe down from the top of the screen to display the Notification panel.

2. Drag down the double dash == icon to see more icons (see the picture below).

To have a robust view of the Quick settings icons, swipe down from the top of the screen using two fingers.

To customize the Quick settings icons:

1. Swipe down from the top of the screen using two fingers.

2. Tap the menu icon ⋮ located at the top of the screen.

3. Tap **Button order.**

4. Tap, hold and drag any of the icons to change their positions.

5. To add an app to the Quick settings panel, drag the app from lower section of the screen (the gray area) to the top section of the screen.

6. To remove an icon from the Quick settings panel, drag the app icon to the lower section of the screen (the gray area).

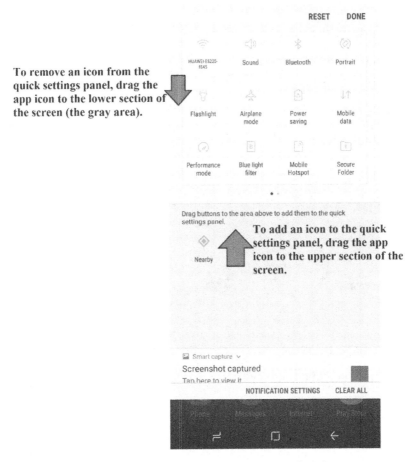

8. Tap **DONE** located at the top of the screen to save the changes.

9. To restore the icons' arrangement to the default arrangement, tap **RESET** and tap **DONE.**

To change the number of app icons that appear in a row/column in Quick settings menu, repeat steps 1 and 2 above. Then select **Button grid** and choose an option.

Customizing Your Phone

You can get more done with your phone by customizing it to match your preference.

Changing Your Phone Language

1. Swipe down from the top of the screen and select settings icon ⚙ . Then scroll down and tap **General management.**

2. Tap **Language and input.**

3. Tap **Language**.

4. Tap **Add language**.

5. If you want to access a more robust list of languages, tap the menu icon ⋮ and tap **All languages**.

6. Select a language from the list. If your chosen language is spoken in more than one country/region, select a country/region for your chosen language.

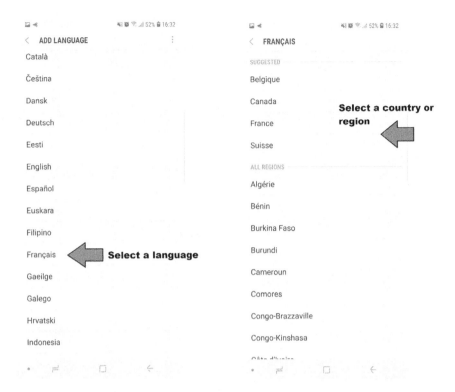

7. Using the v-like icon next to a language, tap and drag your preferred language to the number one position in the language list. Then tap **Done** to set the language as the default language.

8. To delete a language, tap **DELETE** located at the top of the screen and tap the language you want to delete. Then select **DELETE** and tap **OK**. Please see below for details.

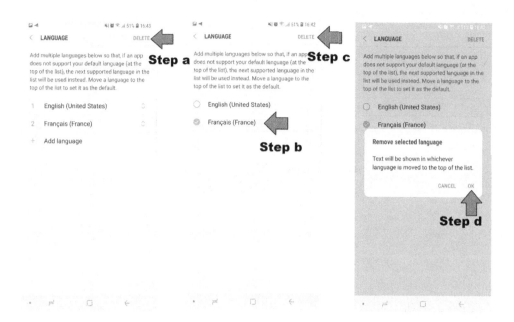

Selecting the Default Keyboard

1. Swipe down from the top of the screen and select settings icon ⚙ . Then scroll down and tap **General management**.
2. Tap **Language and input.**
3. Tap **Default Keyboard** and choose a keyboard. Please note that if you have not downloaded extra keyboards from Google Play Store, you may see only two keyboards.

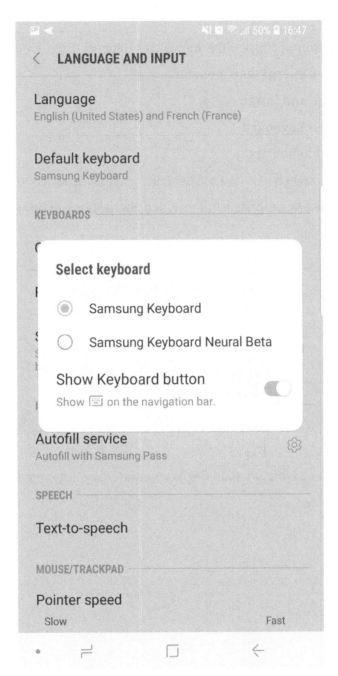

I would advise that you go to Google Play Store to download more keyboard(s). Just open Google Play Store app and search for **Keyboard.** Then choose a beneficial keyboard from the options that appear. After you have downloaded and installed a keyboard, then perform the following actions:

1. Swipe down from the top of the screen and select settings icon ⚙. Then scroll down and tap **General management.**
2. Tap **Language and input.**
3. Tap **On-screen keyboard**
4. Tap **Manage keyboards.**
5. Tap the status switch next to the keyboard you just installed to enable it. In this case, I have just downloaded and installed **SwiftKey Keyboard** from Google Play store.

6. Samsung Galaxy Note 9 would display a cautionary note, read this note and tap **OK** if you agree.

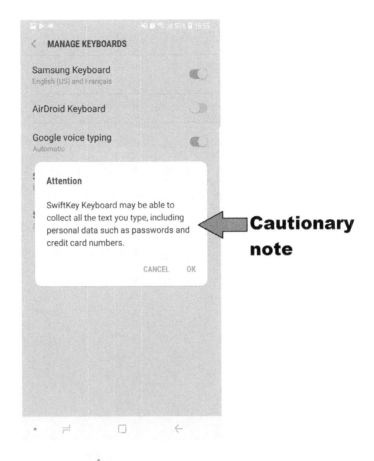

Cautionary note

7. Tap the back button ⟵ until you see **Language and Input** screen. Then tap **Default keyboard** and choose an option.

Your device comes preloaded with Samsung keyboard. To customize this keyboard

to your taste, swipe down from the top of the screen and tap settings icon ⚙️ > **General management** > **Language and input** > **On-Screen Keyboard** > **Samsung keyboard.** Then tap any of the on-screen options. I would advise that you go through these options serially to have the best keyboard experience.

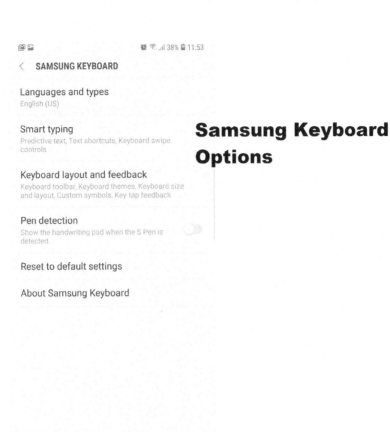

Languages and types
English (US)

Smart typing
Predictive text, Text shortcuts, Keyboard swipe
controls

Keyboard layout and feedback
Keyboard toolbar, Keyboard themes, Keyboard size
and layout, Custom symbols, Key tap feedback

Pen detection
Show the handwriting pad when the S Pen is
detected.

Reset to default settings

About Samsung Keyboard

Samsung Keyboard Options

In addition, you can allow your keyboard to support more languages. To do this, swipe

down from the top of the screen and tap settings icon   **> General management >
Language and input > On-Screen Keyboard > Samsung keyboard > Languages and
types > MANAGE INPUT LANGUAGES.** Then tap the status switch next to all the
languages you want the keyboard to support.

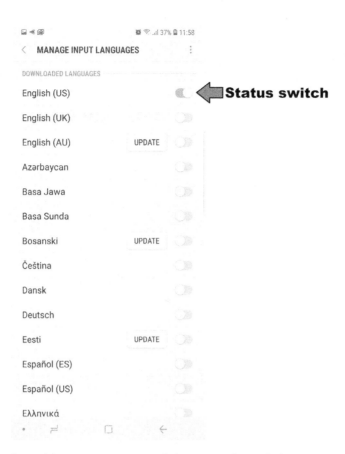

To change your keyboard language to any of the one selected above, swipe the space bar on the virtual keyboard to right or left until you see the language of your choice.

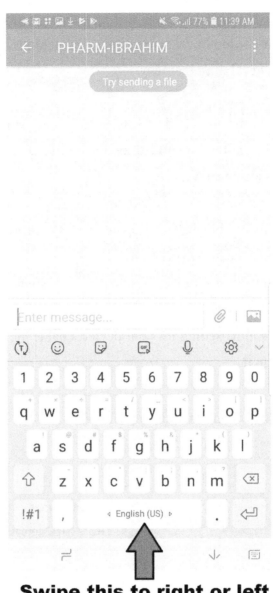

Swipe this to right or left

Set the Current Time and Date

Your device is built to update its time automatically, but you may need to manually set your time for one reason or the other. To manually set the time and date:

1. Swipe down from the top of the screen and select settings icon . Then scroll down and tap **General management.**

2. Tap **Date and time.**

3. To ensure that the time on your device is updated automatically, enable the status switch next to **Automatic date and time.** Please note that when this status switch is enabled, it would appear bold.

4. To set the time on your device manually or prevent your device from updating the time automatically, disable the status switch next to **Automatic date and time**, then edit the time and date as you desire.

5. To manage the time zone settings, disable the status switch next to **Automatic date and time**, then tap **Select time zone.**

6. To use a 24 hours' time setting for your device, enable the status switch next to **Use 24-hour format**.

When the status switch is on, it would appear bold.

< CALENDAR SETTINGS

First day of week
Local default

Show week numbers   ← The status switch is off

Hide declined events   ← The status switch is on

To Control Sounds and Vibrations

1. Swipe down from the top of the screen and select settings icon .

2. Tap **Sounds and vibration** and tap an option.

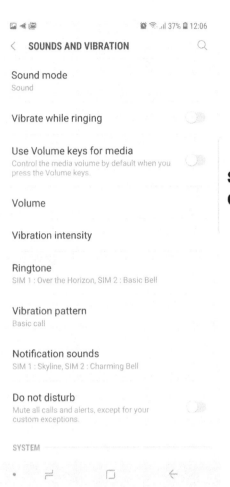

Sound mode
Sound

Vibrate while ringing

Use Volume keys for media
Control the media volume by default when you
press the Volume keys.

Volume

Vibration intensity

Ringtone
SIM 1 : Over the Horizon, SIM 2 : Basic Bell

Vibration pattern
Basic call

Notification sounds
SIM 1 : Skyline, SIM 2 : Charming Bell

Do not disturb
Mute all calls and alerts, except for your
custom exceptions.

SYSTEM

Sound and Vibration Options

3. For example, to mute the sound on your phone, tap **Sound mode**, then tap **Mute**. To mute your phone temporarily, tap the switch next to **Temporary mute**. Then select **Mute duration**.

‹   **SOUND MODE**

○   Sound

○   Vibrate

◉   **Mute** (1 hour remaining)

Temporary mute

Set how long to keep your phone muted before
returning to the previous sound mode (Vibrate).

Mute duration

1 hour

Adjusting the Volume of Your Phone

To adjust the volume of your phone, press the **Volume key**. The volume key is the long
key located at the left side of your phone (when the phone is facing you).

Adjusting the Brightness of the Display

1. Swipe down from the top of the screen using two fingers. Then drag the slider
   under the Quick action icons to adjust the brightness.

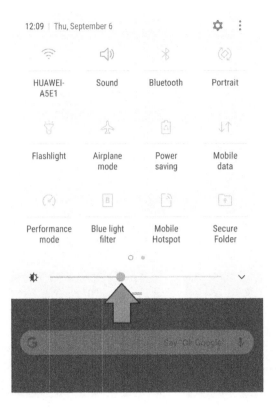

The brightness level of the display will affect how quickly the device consumes battery power. I would advise that you turn it reasonably low if you are very concerned about saving your battery. In addition, using your phone on high brightness for a long time may strain your eye.

In addition, to enable automatic brightness (so that your phone adjusts its brightness based on the lighting conditions of your environment), tap the dropdown arrow. Then tap the switch next to Auto brightness.

Setting a Screen Lock Password or PIN

You can lock your phone by activating the screen lock feature.

📌 Once you set a screen lock, your phone will require an unlock code each time you turn it on or unlock the touch screen.

1. Swipe down from the top of the screen and tap the settings icon ⚙.
2. Tap **Lock screen** and tap **Screen lock type**.
3. Tap a screen lock type you like.
4. If you choose **Password or PIN**, then enter the **password/PIN** you desire and follow the on-screen instructions to complete the setup. In addition, you may choose **Pattern** or **Swipe.** If you don't want a lock screen, tap **None.**

💡 You may also use your fingerprint, intelligent scan or iris to unlock your phone. More on this on page 139.

Adjusting Font Size/Style on Your Phone

You can change the font on your phone to a bigger or smaller font by following the steps below:

1. Swipe down from the top of the screen and tap settings icon   .
2. Tap **Display**.
3. Select **Font and screen zoom**.
4. To adjust the font size, drag the slider next to **Font Size**. You would see the preview of font size at the upper part of the screen.
5. To change the font style, select a font under the **Font Style** tab.
6. Tap **Done** to save the changes.

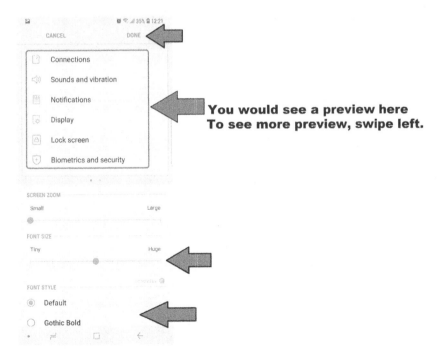

If you want to see your phone in a new way, simply change the font style following the method described above.

Changing the Display Size

You can change the display on your phone to a bigger or smaller display. When the display is bigger, the items on the screen should appear bigger. When the display is smaller, the item on the screen should appear smaller. To change the display size, follow the steps below:

1. Swipe down from the top of the screen and tap settings icon .
2. Tap **Display**.
3. Select **Font and screen zoom**
4. To adjust the display size, drag the slider next to **Screen Zoom**. You would see the preview of the display size at the upper part of the screen.
5. Tap **Done** to save the changes.

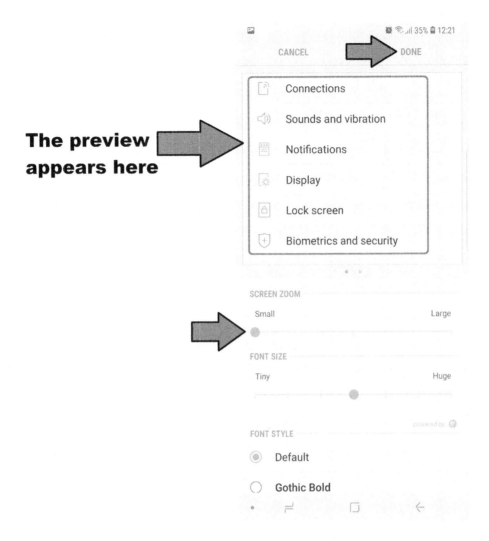

The preview appears here

Smart Lock

Smart lock allows you to lock your device like a pro. This feature allows you to quickly lock and unlock your phone.

To use smart lock:

1. Swipe down from the top of the screen and select settings icon .
2. Tap **Lock screen**.

3. If you have not set up a secure lock before, tap **Screen lock type**, choose a PIN and follow the on-screen instructions to set up this lock type. Please skip this step if you have already set up a secure lock.

4. Tap **Smart Lock.** You would only be able to select Smart Lock after you have set up a screen lock type.

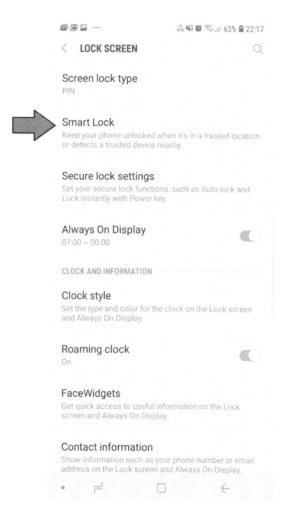

5. Enter your screen lock information and tap **Next**.

6. Pick an option on the screen (the options include **On-body detection, Trusted places, Trusted devices** and **Voice Match.**) Then follow the on-screen instructions to complete the setup.

To remove or deactivate a smart lock option:

1. Repeat steps 1 to 4 above.
2. Pick a smart lock type.
3. Tap an option corresponding to what you want to do. For example, to remove "Trusted places," tap the current address/place and select **Delete** or **Edit Address** (located at the top of the screen).

📌 Please note that using smart lock may allow a third party to easily access your phone. For example, if you set up "trusted places", your phone might unlock while in these places (or around them) even when you don't want it to unlock.

In addition, On-body detection can't distinguish between you and someone else. This means if someone else takes your phone while it is unlocked, the person might be able to access your data because the phone might remain unlocked.

💡 You can use **Trusted places** option to automatically unlock your phone while at home and automatically lock your phone while at work or outside the home. All you need to do to achieve this is to set up your home as a trusted place.

In addition, to use "Trusted places", you might need to enable location (if you have not done so).

To activate location services:

1. Swipe down from the top of the screen and select the settings icon .
2. Tap **Connection**.
3. Tap **Location**.
4. Next to the switch under **Location**, select **On**.

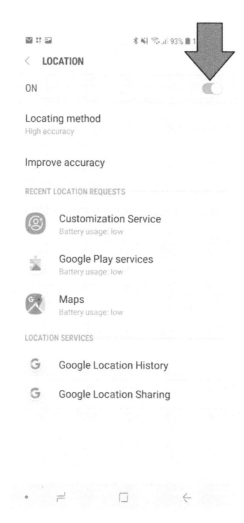

Entering a text

You can enter a text by selecting characters on the virtual keypad or by speaking words into the microphone using a voice command app.

To enter a text:

1. Enter a text by selecting the corresponding letters, symbols or numbers.

2. You can use any of the following keys:

Please note that the on-screen keyboard on your phone may be different from the one shown below. This is because the on-screen keyboard you see depends on the text input field you select. The one shown below is the one you should see when you want to compose a text message.

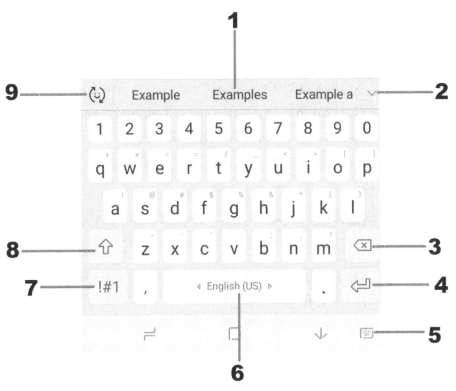

Number	Function
1.	**Predictive text bar** The phone has an auto replace feature and as you type, your phone will give you text suggestions, the most likely suggestions would appear in blue on the predictive text bar. To use the suggestion that appears in blue (the suggestion that appears at the center), tap the space bar. To use a different suggestion, tap on it. Please be informed that you can disable this auto replace feature, to do this, please see page 136.

2.	Tap on this to see more predictive texts, settings or disable the auto replace option.
3.	Clear your input/backspace
4.	Start a new line.
5.	Tap this icon to select a new keyboard type. If you don't want to see this icon again, tap this icon and tap the status switch next to **Show Keyboard button**. To show this icon again, go to **Settings** ⚙ > **General management** and tap **Language and input**. Tap the status switch next to **Show Keyboard button**.
6.	**Space bar**: you can swipe right or left to switch between input languages. To add input language, go to page 119.
7.	Switch between Number/Symbol mode and ABC mode
8.	Change case
9.	**Option tab**: when you tap this button, you will gain access to a list of icons/functions.

When you tap the option tab you will gain access to the following:

1. **Keyboard settings:** Tap this to access the keyboard settings.
2. **Voice input**: Enter text by voice.
3. **One-handed keyboard**: Tap this to be able to control the virtual keyboard using one hand. When you tap the **One-handed keyboard** button, you will see a keyboard that looks like the one below.

Tap this to exit one-handed keyboard

Tap this to move keyboard to the left

4. **Clipboard:** Tap this to add an item from the clipboard. After using an item on the clipboard, tap the arrow icon ↓ (located at the bottom of the screen) to exit.

5. **Handwriting to text**: Tap this to access handwriting-to-text feature. Then use the S Pen or your finger to write on the screen.

6. **Option button:** Tap this to switch to predictive texts.

If you select any of the icons described above and you wish to unselect it so as to show the virtual keyboard, simply tap the icon again.

To learn how to manage the on-screen keyboard, please see page 118. When you select two or more languages, you can switch between the input languages by swiping to the left or right on the space key.

By default, you may notice that Samsung automatically replaces your typed word with another one (a corrected one) when you press the space bar. While this option is cool, it may be unwanted sometimes, to disable this function, go to **Settings** ⚙ > **General management** > **Language and input** > **On-Screen Keyboard** > **Samsung keyboard** > **Smart typing** > **Auto replace.** Then tap the status switch next to **English** (or your default language) to disable it.

Alternatively, you may disable auto replace by tapping the **v** icon on the virtual keyboard. Then tap the status switch next to **Auto replace**.

Copy and Paste a Text

While entering or reading a text, you can use the copy and paste options. To do this:

1. Tap and hold a word to display copy options. The icons below will show up after selecting a text or texts.

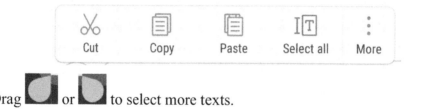

2. Drag ◖ or ◗ to select more texts.

3. Select **Copy** icon to copy or select **Cut** icon to cut the text onto the clipboard.

4. In another application or where you want to paste the text, tap and hold the text input field.

5. Select **Paste** icon to insert the text from the clipboard into the text input field. You can also tap the more icon More , then tap the clipboard icon to access the clipboard for more paste options.

Using the Voice Typing

1. Tap the option tab and select .

2. Say your texts. Your device types as you speak.

3. To pause the voice typing, tap .

4. To manage the voice typing option, tap ⚙ . Alternatively, swipe down from the top of the screen and tap **Settings** ⚙ > **General management** and tap **Language and input**. Tap **On-Screen keyboard** and tap **Google voice typing**.

5. To delete, tap the backspace button ⌫ .

6. To exit the voice typing, tap the arrow icon ↓ (located at the bottom of the screen).

Using The Special Features

Samsung Galaxy Note 9 comes with special features that makes it distinct. I will now explain how to use these features.

Using the Fingerprint Feature

One of the cool features on Samsung Galaxy Note 9 is the fingerprint scanner. This allows you to unlock applications without entering boring passwords.

💡 You can use your biometrics to unlock websites and apps. To learn how to get started, go to page 249.

Registering your Fingerprint

Before you can start using your fingerprint on the device, you will need to first register your fingerprint. You have the chance of registering up to four fingerprints. In addition, you also have the option of registering a password as a backup.

To do this:

1. Swipe down from the top of the screen and select the settings icon .
2. Tap **Biometrics and security**.
3. Tap **Fingerprint scanner**.
4. Read the on-screen tips and tap **Continue**.
5. Tap an alternative lock method and follow the prompts. You will need this alternative lock method in some occasions. If you have set a lock screen before, then you just need to enter the lock PIN/Password/Pattern.

6. Place one of your fingers on the fingerprint reader located under the phone camera at the back of the phone, then lift it when the fingerprint is detected and read. You may need to repeat this several times.

Fingerprint scanner

7. To add another fingerprint, tap **Add** and follow the prompts.
8. When you are done adding your fingerprints, tap **Done.**

Renaming Fingerprints

1. Swipe down from the top of the screen and select settings icon .
2. Tap **Biometrics and security**.
3. Tap **Fingerprint scanner**.
4. Unlock the screen using the preset screen lock method and tap **Done/Next**.
5. Tap the fingerprint you want to rename. For example, tap **Fingerprint 1.**

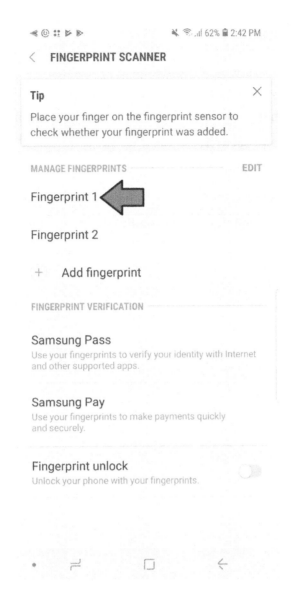

6. Enter a new name and tap **Rename**.

When renaming your fingerprint, make sure you use the name of the finger you registered. For example, you can use the name **Index finger** or **Forefinger**. This prevents unnecessary confusion.

Deleting Fingerprints

1. Swipe down from the top of the screen and select the settings icon .

2. Tap **Biometrics and security**.

3. Tap **Fingerprint scanner**.

4. Unlock the screen using the preset screen lock method and tap **Done/Next**.

5. Touch and hold the fingerprint you want to delete and tap **Remove**.

Setting a Screen Lock with Fingerprint

You can lock the screen with your fingerprint instead of using a pattern, PIN or password.

1. Swipe down from the top of the screen and select settings icon .

2. Tap **Lock screen**.

3. Tap **Screen lock type**.

4. Unlock the screen using the preset screen lock method and tap **Next/Done**.

5. Tap the status switch next to **Fingerprint.**

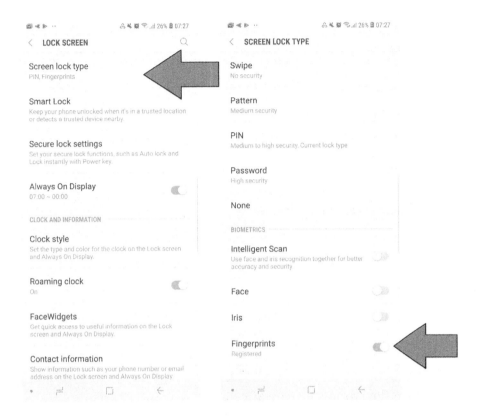

Using Fingerprints to Sign In to Accounts

Apart from using your fingerprint to unlock your device, you can also use it to access online features.

1. Swipe down from the top of the screen and select settings icon .

2. Tap **Biometrics and security**.

3. Tap **Fingerprint scanner**. Unlock the screen using the preset screen lock method, then do any of the following:

a. Tap **Samsung Pass** to access your online accounts/apps using your fingerprint. To get started with this feature, just tap Samsung Pass and follow the prompts.

b. Tap **Samsung Pay** to use your fingerprint for secured and fast payments with the Samsung Pay app. To get started with this feature, just tap Samsung Pay and follow the prompts. Samsung Pay may not be available in some locations in the world.

c. Tap the switch next to **Fingerprint unlock** to enable or disable fingerprint security.

Troubleshooting the Fingerprint Scanner

If the fingerprint scanner is not responding, try any of the following:

1. Remove any phone case that may be covering the fingerprint reader located at the back of the phone.

2. Ensure that you are not using the tip of your fingerprint. Make sure to cover the entire Fingerprint reader with your finger.

3. If your finger has scars, try using another finger. This is because your device may not recognize fingerprints that are affected by wrinkles or scars.

4. Ensure the finger you registered with is used.

5. Make sure that your finger and the surface of the fingerprint scanner are clean and dry.

Iris Scanner

You can lock and unlock your phone using your iris.

1. Swipe down from the top of the screen and select settings icon .

2. Tap **Biometrics and security**.

3. Tap **Iris scanner**. You may need to setup an alternative lock screen method or enter your lock screen information if you have already setup a lock screen.

4. Read the on-screen tips and tap **Next/OK/Continue**.

   Please note that it is recommended that you keep the screen at least 20 cm away from your face to protect your eyes when using iris recognition. In addition, if you have any symptom linked to epileptic conditions, it is advised you see your doctor before using the iris scanner.

5. Hold the phone 25 to 35 cm from your face. Make sure you are not wearing glasses. Follow the prompts to complete the registration.

6. After the registration, you will see some information telling you more about the Iris scanner. Read this information and tap the next icon 〉 located at the bottom of the screen. Finally, tap **OK** to go to Iris setting page.

SELECT A MASK

Add your own style to iris scanning. Go to Settings
> Biometrics and security > Iris Scanner > Preview
screen mask.

7. If prompted, tap **Not Now** if you are not ready to use iris unlock or select **Turn On** to use iris unlock.

8. On the iris settings page, tap an option to enable/disable it. To know what each option stands for, read the information under the option.

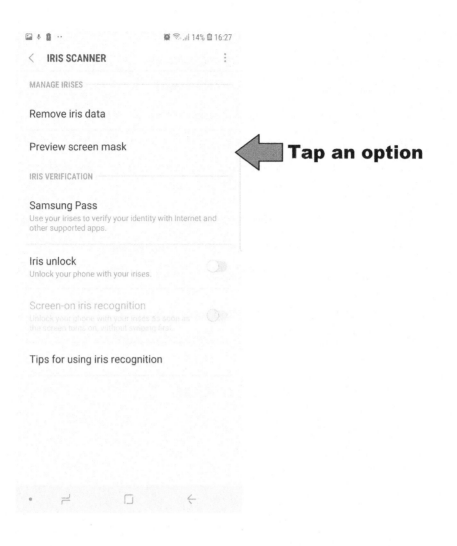

IRIS SCANNER

MANAGE IRISES

Remove iris data

Preview screen mask

Tap an option

IRIS VERIFICATION

Samsung Pass
Use your irises to verify your identity with Internet and other supported apps.

Iris unlock
Unlock your phone with your irises.

Screen-on iris recognition
Unlock your phone with your irises as soon as the screen turns on, without swiping first.

Tips for using iris recognition

9. To remove Iris data, tap **Remove iris data** and tap **Remove**.

10. To get tips for using iris recognition, tap **Tips for using iris recognition**.

Troubleshooting the Iris Scanner

If the Iris scanner is not responding, try any of the following:

1. Remove any screen protector that may be covering the iris scanner, LED sensor, or proximity sensor located above your screen.

2. Ensure that you are not wearing glasses.

3. Ensure that you are not trying to use the iris scanner under the direct sunlight.

4. Ensure that you hold the phone between 25 and 35 cm from your face.

5. Ensure you hold the phone to the level of your face/eyes.

Intelligent Scan

Intelligent scan combines face and iris scanning for better results. You would need to register your face and irises to use intelligent scan.

To use intelligent scan:

1. Swipe down from the top of the screen and select the settings icon .

2. Tap **Biometrics and security**.

3. Tap **Intelligent Scan**. You may need to setup an alternative lock screen method or enter your lock screen information if you have already setup a lock screen.

4. Read the on-screen tips and tap **Next/OK**.

5. Read the on-screen information and tap **Continue**.

6. Then carefully follow the onscreen instructions to set up intelligent scan.

7. On the Intelligent scan settings page, tap an option to enable/disable it. To know what each option stands for, read the information under the option.

8. To enable intelligent scan unlock, tap the status switch next to **Intelligent Scan unlock**.

9. To remove your face and iris data, tap the status switch next to **Remove face and iris data**.

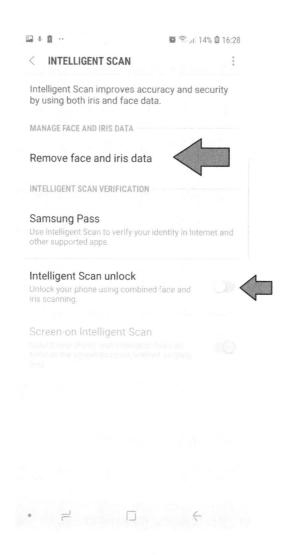

Water Resistance

Another feature that makes Samsung Galaxy Note 9 unique is the water resistivity. You don't have to worry that your phone is going to get wet when you are drenched by the rain or inside a bathroom. To know more about water resistivity, please go to page 36.

The S Pen

One of the features that make using Galaxy Note 9 very interesting is the stylus pen. You can use S pen as you use a normal writing pen. In this section of the guide, I would be telling you how to use your S pen like a pro.

Removing the S Pen

To remove the S Pen:

1. Push the S Pen inward until it pops out of the device.

S Pen

2. Then gently slide the S Pen out using the notch at the end of the S Pen.

S Pen Layout

Number	Function
1.	**S Pen Head:** Push this head inward to remove the S Pen from the Note 9.
2.	**S Pen Body**
3.	**S Pen Button**: This button allows you to use S Pen in a special way. To learn more about S Pen button, go to page 163.
4.	**S Pen Tip**: This allows you to write on the surface of your device. This tip is replaceable.

You may customize the S Pen features as you like. To do this, swipe down from the

top of the screen and tap **Settings** > **Advanced Features > S Pen.**

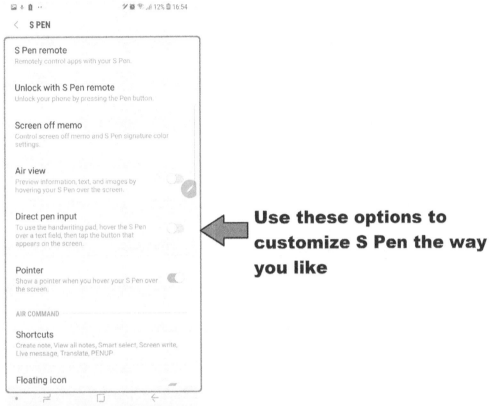

Use these options to customize S Pen the way you like

S Pen and Air View

One of the cool features with the S pen is the Air View. Air View allows you to view more information about an item just by hovering your S Pen over it.

For example, you can hover the S Pen over a date in your calendar app to preview the events for that day. In addition, you can hover over an icon to view the icon's name or description. The trick is to hover your S Pen tip over whatever you want to learn more about.

Please note that the preview function may not be available in some cases.

In addition, please note that you may need to enable Air View. To do this, swipe down

from the top of the screen and tap **Settings** **> Advanced Features > S Pen >Air view**

⚡ 📵 📶 12% 🔋 16:59

‹ **S PEN**

Air view
On

Direct pen input
To use the handwriting pad, hover the S Pen
over a text field, then tap the button that
appears on the screen.

Pointer
Show a pointer when you hover your S Pen over
the screen.

AIR COMMAND

Shortcuts
Create note, View all notes, Smart select, Screen write,
Live message, Translate, PENUP

Floating icon
Show an Air command icon that you can move
around the screen.

REMOVAL

When S Pen is removed
Open Air command

Alarm
Sound an alarm if you walk away with your
phone without inserting the S Pen and the
screen is off.

S Pen and Air Command

Air Commands are set of options that appear when you remove the S Pen from your device. These options give more functionalities to the S Pen.

To access the Air Command:

4. Remove the S Pen from its holder by pushing it inwards and letting it pop out. The Air Command menu will open automatically. If the Air command does not open automatically or if you have already taken the S Pen out, tap the Air command icon (located at the middle edge of the screen) to access the Air Command. Another way to open the Air Command is to hold the S Pen near the screen so that the pointer appears, then press the S Pen button once. In addition, you could move the Air command icon to another part of the screen, simply tap and drag it to a new location.

The screenshot below shows the Air Command options.

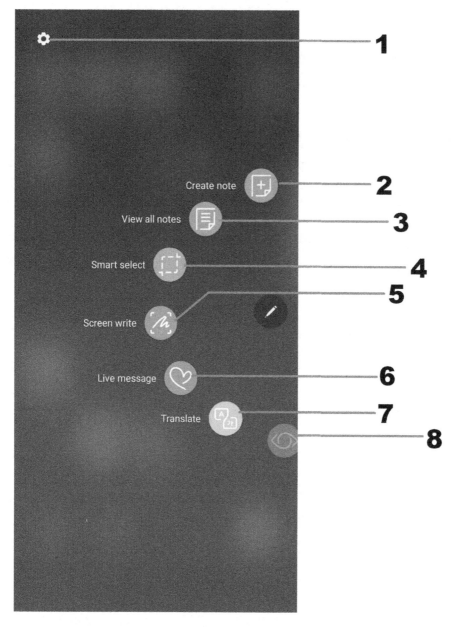

1. **Air Command Settings:** This allows you to customize S Pen settings.

2. **Create Note**: Tap this using your S Pen to launch the Note app. You could go to Samsung Notes to have a more robust experience. To do this, click the menu icon

   ⋮ and select **Go to Samsung Notes**.

3. **View all notes**: Tap this to access all your notes. To edit any of your notes, tap the note and tap **Edit** located at the top of the screen. To know what each editing icon stands for, simply hover the S Pen over the editing icon. Please note that you would need to enable Air View to use this option. To enable Air View, see page 151.

To categorize your note, open the note and click on **Uncategorized**. Then select **Add category**, enter a name and select **Create**.

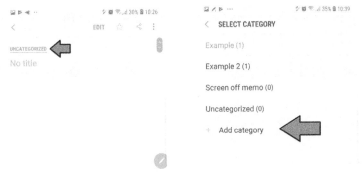

If you want to add the note to an existing category, simply tap the category.

4. **Smart Select**: Smart Select allows you to extract parts of an image. You can use this feature to extract out texts from an image. To use Smart select:

a. Navigate to the page you want to capture, then tap **Smart select** using the S Pen. Tap **Confirm** if you agree with the terms and conditions. If you don't agree, you might be unbale to use Smart select.

b. Tap a shape at the top of the screen. In this example, the **Rectangle** shape is selected.

c. Using the S Pen, draw the chosen shape over what you want to select. In our example, we would draw a rectangle around the area we wish to select.

d. Tap **Auto select**, **Extract text** or **Pin to screen**.

e. Tap **Save** (if needed). The saved image should be in your gallery.

5. **Screen Write:** This allows you to capture screenshots and write on them.

6. **Live message:** Tap this to write and share live messages.

7. **Translate:** When this is selected, hover the S Pen over a word to see it translated into another language. To use the translation feature:

a. While on the Air Command screen, tap **Translate**.

b. Tap the Source and Target languages to change them to the desired language(s).

Target language

Source language

Tap this icon to close
this feature

c. Hover the S Pen over a word to see its translation.

d. Tap the voice icon 🔊 to hear the word pronounced in the source language.

e. Tap **X** to close this feature.

8. **Bixby Vision:** Tap this to access Bixby Vision (see page 224). Then hover the S Pen over an item you want to know more about. Thereafter, select whether you want extract text, scan a QR code or you want to know more about an image.

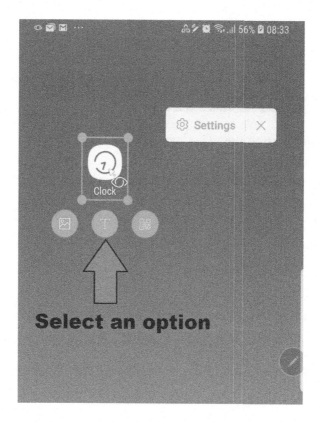

You may want to know how to access **Add shortcuts** tab if it is not showing. To access **Add shortcuts** tab; while on the Air Command page, swipe up using the S Pen.

If "Add Shortcuts" is not showing up, swipe up the screen using the S Pen to bring it into view

Add shortcuts allows you to add or remove items from the Air Command menu and rearrange the Air Command icons. To add a shortcut:

    a. While on the Air Command screen, tap **Add shortcuts.**

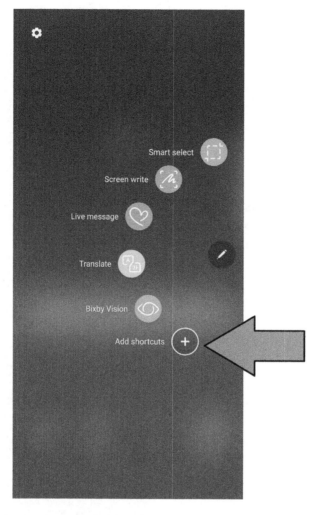

b. Tap the apps you would like to add.

c. To delete an app shortcut, tap the minus icon next to the app you want to delete.

d. In addition, you can rearrange the Air Command icons. To do this, using the S pen, long tap an icon, then move it to a new location.

e. Tap the back button to save the changes.

💡 You can quickly remove an icon from the Air Command screen. To do this, using the S pen, tap and hold an icon and drag it to **Remove** located at the top of the screen.

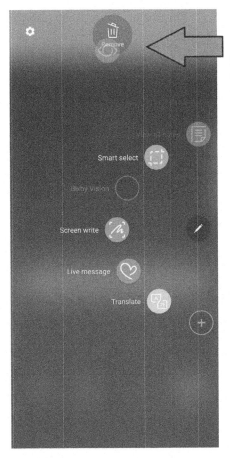

Using the S Pen, tap and drag the icon you want to remove to the top of the screen. In this example, I am trying to remove Bixby Vision icon.

Using the S Pen and the handwriting panel

You can write something on the writing field of supported apps and your device will automatically convert your written words to text. To do this:

1. Open an app and tap the text field (where you want to type information). The virtual keyboard appears, tap the option icon 🙂 (if needed) and select Handwriting to text icon 🖊 .

2. Begin to write in the writing field that appears. Your entries would be converted to text when you lift up the S Pen.

3. To delete a text, strikethrough the handwritten text. In addition, you can edit the converted text using your keyboard.

4. To go back to the ABC virtual keyboard, tap ⌣ (if needed), then tap the Handwriting to text icon ✏ again.

S Pen and Screen Off Memo

Quick memos allow you to write without turning your device on.

To create a screen off memo:

1. Detach the S Pen while the screen is off to access screen off memo. To make your screen go off, press the power key once. If you have detached the S Pen already, while the screen is off, tap the screen while pressing the S Pen button to access the screen off memo.

2. Write on the screen.

3. To go to another page or open a new page, tap the new page icon located at the bottom of the screen.

4. Tap **SAVE IN NOTES** located at the top of the screen to save your memo to the Samsung Notes app. Alternatively, to save the memo, just replace the S Pen into its slot.

5. To change the pen thickness, tap the pen icon and pick an option.

6. To pin a note to **Always On Display**, tap the pin icon , then tap **Pin To Always On Display**. Please note that you would need to enable Always On Display to see the pin icon. To learn more about Always on Display, go to page 168.

7. To erase a word, select the eraser icon and move the tip of your S pen over what you want to erase. Alternatively, to erase a word, press the S Pen button and move the tip of the S pen over whatever you want to erase.

8. To delete a note, tap the back button , then select **Discard**.

If not enabled, please note that you may need to enable screen off memo to use it. To do this, swipe down from the top of the screen and tap the settings icon > **Advanced Features > S Pen > Screen off memo**.

Using the S Pen Remote

The S Pen allows you to control your phone from a distance when you press and hold down the S Pen button.

S Pen Button

To customize what happens when you press and hold down the S Pen button:

1. Swipe down from the top of the screen and tap settings icon .

2. Tap **Advanced Features**.

3. Tap **S Pen**.

4. Tap **S Pen remote**.

5. Tap **Hold Down Pen Button To**

6. Tap an application from the list.

7. To open the app you have selected in step 6, press and hold down the S Pen button.

8. In addition, you can control some specific apps (like Voice Recorder) when you single press or double press the S Pen button while these apps are opened. To control how single/double pressing S Pen button affects each app, tap **Single press/Double press** next to the app you want to control and pick an option. In the picture below, we want to adjust the single/double press settings for Voice Recorder.

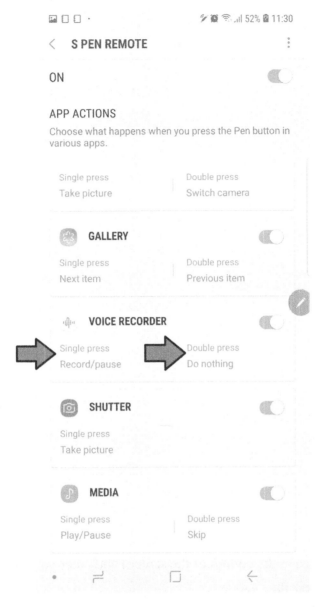

You could use the S Pen to unlock your phone if it locks while you are using your S Pen. To do so, simply press the S Pen button once. Please note that you might need to enable this option to use it. Go to **Settings** > **Advanced Features > S Pen > Unlock with S Pen remote**. Then select **Unlock with S Pen remote**.

Then tap OK (located at the bottom of the screen) and enter your screen lock information. Click **Next** to save the changes.

S Pen Settings

S Pen settings allows you to use S Pen like a pro. I would advise you go to these settings whenever you think of using S Pen in a new way.

To access the S pen settings:

1. Swipe down from the top of the screen and tap settings icon .

2. Tap **Advanced Features**.

3. Tap **S Pen**.

4. Pick an option. I would advise you go through the S Pen settings one by one to get familiar with them.

Changing the tip of your S Pen

You can replace the tip of the S Pen with the included pen tip removal tool.

To change the pen tip:

1. Grasp the pen tip with the included tweezers (the metal-like object included with your phone) and pull it straight out.

2. Insert the base of the new tip into the pen opening and push it in until it locks into place.

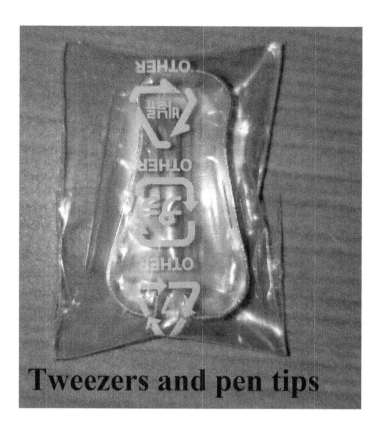

Tweezers and pen tips

Using the Always On Feature

The Always On feature allows you to display information, such as a clock, calendar, or image, on the screen when it is turned off. Seeing the time even when the screen is off is cool.

To use this feature:

1. Swipe down from the top of the screen and select settings icon ⚙.
2. Tap **Lock screen**.
3. Scroll down and tap **Always on display**.

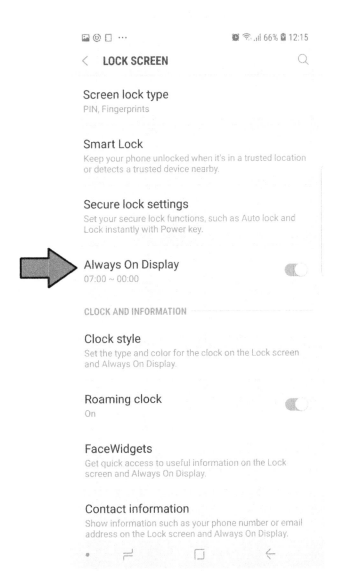

4. Tap On/Off switch to enable or disable Always on Display.

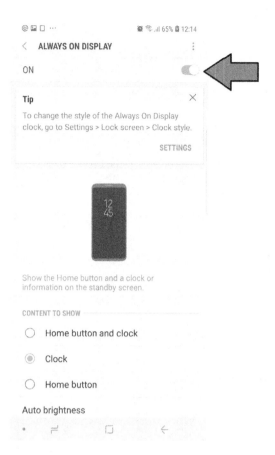

When you enable **Always on Display**, you can access the following:

a. **Content to show**: This feature allows you to choose the content to show when the screen is off. See the screenshot below.

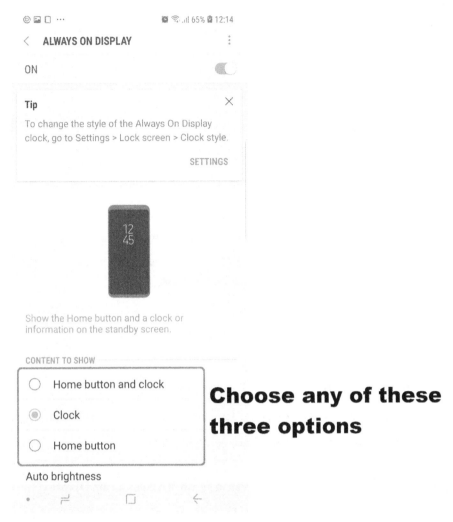

Choose any of these three options

b. **Auto brightness**: Use this tab to control the brightness level of the clock on the Always on Display screen. Please note that choosing a high brightness level may drain the battery of your phone faster.

c. **Show Always**: When this is enabled, the Always on Display is active every time. To customize when Always on Display will be active, tap the status switch next to **Show Always** and set a schedule.

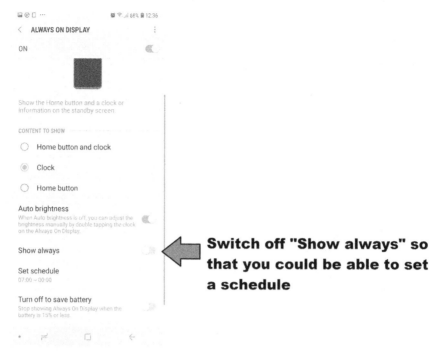

ALWAYS ON DISPLAY

ON

Show the Home button and a clock or information on the standby screen.

CONTENT TO SHOW

○ Home button and clock

◉ Clock

○ Home button

Auto brightness
When Auto brightness is off, you can adjust the brightness manually by double tapping the clock on the Always On Display.

Show always

Set schedule
07:00 ~ 00:00

Turn off to save battery
Stop showing Always On Display when the battery is 15% or less.

Switch off "Show always" so that you could be able to set a schedule

d. **Turn off to save battery**: When this option is enabled, "Always On Display" will be switched off when the battery is 15% or less.

e. **About Always On Display**: Tap this to view the current software version, update the app and check license information.

Changing the Clock style/Calendar style/Image on "Always On Display"

You can choose the clock style, calendar style, image, or Edge clock to be displayed when "Always On Display" is active. To do this:

1. Swipe down from the top of the screen and select settings icon ⚙.

2. Tap **Lock screen**.

3. Tap **Clock style**

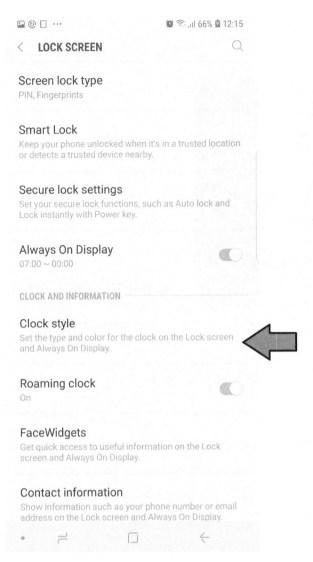

4. Scroll through the available clock style/calendar style/image thumbnails and choose one. If clock/calendar style thumbnails are not showing, tap **Clock style** (located at the bottom of the screen).

Tap Done to save the changes

**Scroll through the available clock/
calendar style by swiping through
the thumbnails**

**Tap "Clock style" if the thumbnails
are not showing up**

5. Tap **Color** and select color of your choice.

6. Tap **Done** located at the top of the screen to effect changes. Note that you may not be able to choose a clock, image or calendar to display if you choose **Home button** only under Content to Show (see page 170).

7. To change the clock style on the Lock Screen, tap Lock Screen (see the picture below) and choose a clock. Then tap **Done** to save the changes.

Tap "Lock Screen" to change the clock style on the lock screen

You can enable your phone to show you today's schedule and next alarm even when your screen is locked. To do this go to settings > **Lock screen** > **FaceWidgets**. Then tap the status switches next to **Today's schedule** and **Next alarm.**

To check your alarm or schedule, double tap around the middle of the screen to bring out the scrolling icons (< >) and tap > or < to see your event/alarm.

Fast Battery Charging

One of the cool features on Samsung Galaxy Note 9 is Fast Battery Charging. With this feature, your device can get 50% of battery power in about 45-55 minutes. You can learn how to use this feature by going to page 20

Using the Edge Screen on Samsung Galaxy Note 9

The Edge screen transforms the way you handle Samsung Galaxy Note 9. Edge panels can be used to access apps, tasks, contacts and more.

Please note that the Edge panel might be disabled by default, to enable Edge panel, go to Settings > Display > Edge Screen. Then tap the indicator switch next to Edge panels.

To access the Edge panel:

1. Drag the Edge panel handle located at the Edge of the screen. To access more Edge items, swipe again from the edge of the screen. If you are using the Edge panel for the first time, follow the onscreen instructions to get started.

2. To access Edge panel settings, tap the settings icon located at the bottom of the screen (this setting icon appears while viewing the Edge options).

Using the Edge Panel

The Edge Panel allows you to use the Edge screen in a special way. To manage the Edge panel:

1. Swipe down from the top of the screen and select the settings icon ![settings]. Then tap **Display** tab**.**
2. Scroll down and tap **Edge Screen**.
3. Tap **Edge Panels**.

4. To download exciting panels, tap the menu icon ⋮ (located at the top of the screen) and select **Download**.

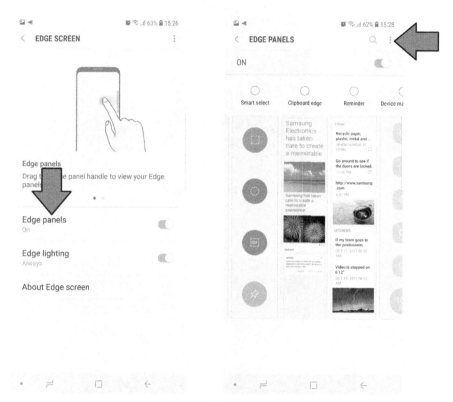

Tap the Edge panel you want to download. Then tap **Install** to download and install your

chosen panel. To go back to the Edge panel screen, tap the back button ← . To see your newly installed panel, navigate to the **Edge Panels** screen and swipe left.

ON

Swipe left to see newly installed panel. In this case the newly installed panel is "Recent Calls".

5. To uninstall an Edge panel that you don't like, tap the menu icon ⋮ located at the top of the Edge panel's screen and select **Uninstall**. Then select the minus icon (--) located at the top of the panel you want to uninstall. When prompted, tap **OK.** Please note that the uninstall button may not be available if you have not installed any Edge panel from the Edge panel store.

6. There are some Edge panels that allow you to edit them. To edit an editable panel, just tap **EDIT** next to the panel you want to edit. *Please note that you may need to enable a panel before you can edit it. To learn how to enable a panel, please go to step 7.*

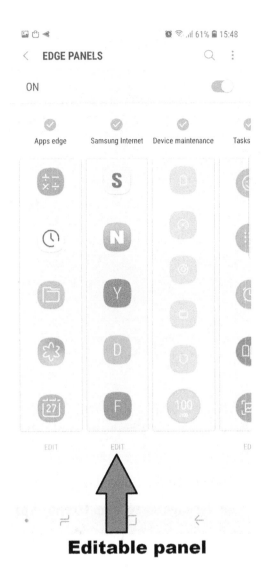

Editable panel

Then tap and hold an item and move it to the Edge screen. To remove an item, tap the minus icon. To rearrange the icons, tap and drag the icon(s) to a new location. See the picture below.

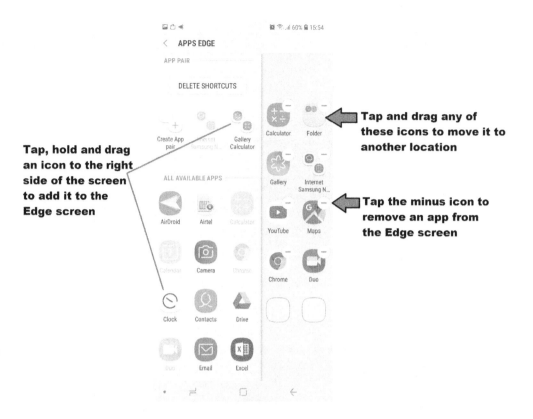

Although, *Apps Edge* has been used in the example above, you can also manage People Edge in similar way. In addition, please note that there is a maximum number of items you can add to the Edge screen.

To create "app pair" on the edge screen, tap **Create App pair**, select the two apps you like and tap **DONE** to save the changes. To move the app at the bottom to the top and vice versa, tap **Switch**. To delete your selection and select another apps, tap **Clear**.

7. To enable an Edge panel or select the Edge panel that you want to see on the Edge screen, simply tap/tick the circle on top of the panel. To disable/remove a panel, simply unselect the circle.

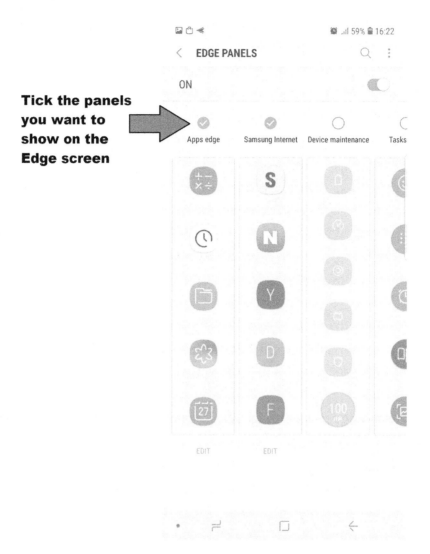

Tick the panels you want to show on the Edge screen

8. To disable Edge panels, tap the status switch next to **ON**. Please note that when you disable Edge Panel, the Edge handle would disappear.

If you download many Edge panels, you may not be able to access all these panels at once on your Edge screen. You may not be able to use more than nine Edge panels at once. To select the Edge panels that you want to access, simply follow step 7 above. In addition, to view all the Edge panels you have enabled at once, swipe Edge Panel handle and tap the list icon .

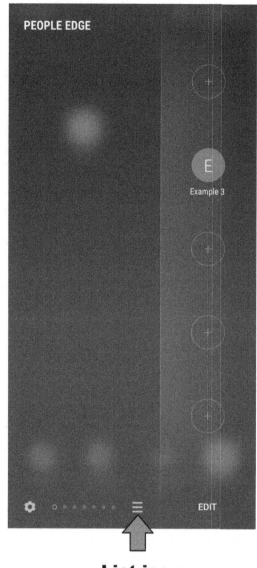

List icon

Using the Edge Lighting

This feature allows you to set the Edge screen to light up when you receive calls or notifications.

1. Swipe down from the top of the screen and select settings icon . Tap **Display** tab**.**

2. Scroll down and tap **Edge Screen**.

3. Tap **Edge Lighting**.

4. Tap the switch next to **ON**. The switch will appear bold when enabled.

5. Select when to show the Edge lighting. If you want Edge Lighting to be active every time, then select **Always**.

6. Tap **Manage notifications** to select those apps that will work with Edge Lighting.

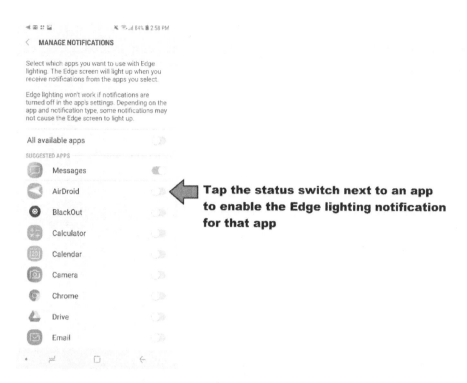

It appears that not all notifications may be received as Edge lighting.

To customize the color, the size or the transparency of the Edge lighting, tap the **Edge lighting style** and use the on-screen buttons to customize the edge lighting. Then tap **Apply** to save the changes.

Tap this to save the changes

Use these options to customize Edge lighting

Reordering the Edge Screen Panel

1. Swipe down from the top of the screen and select the settings icon ⚙. Tap **Display** tab**.**

2. Scroll down and tap **Edge Screen**.

3. Tap **Edge Panels**.

4. Tap the menu ⋮ icon located at the top of the screen and tap **REORDER**.

5. Tap and hold the reorder icon (<>) on an Edge screen panel and drag it to the desired position. Make sure that the panels you use most are the first 3 or 4 panels so that you can access them faster.

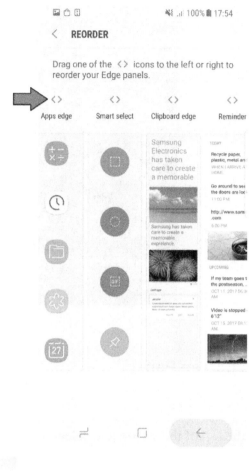

6. Tap back icon ← to save the changes.

Managing the Edge Panel Handle Settings/Changing the Edge Panel Location

Edge panel handle settings allows you to change the position of Edge panel and more.

1. Swipe down from the top of the screen and select settings icon ⚙ . Tap **Display** tab.

2. Scroll down and tap **Edge Screen**.

3. Tap **Edge Panels**.

4. Tap the menu icon ⋮ located at the top of the screen and select **Edge panel handle.**

5. Under **Position** tab, tap the side you would like the panel to appear on.

6. To change the size of Edge panel, drag the slider next to **SIZE**.

7. To change the transparency of Edge panel, drag the slider next to **Transparency.**

8. To move the Edge panel handle to another part of the screen, tap and drag the Edge handle anchor (the small V-shape icon).

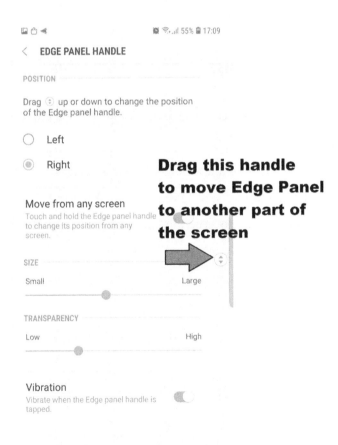

Using People Edge

People Edge gives you the opportunity to quickly access your favorite contacts from Edge Panel.

To manage People Edge:

1. Swipe down from the top of the screen and select settings icon . Tap **Display** tab.

2. Scroll down and tap **Edge Screen**.

3. Tap **Edge Panels**.

4. Tap **EDIT** under **People Edge**. If you can't see the **Edit** button, then **People Edge** is disabled. To enable **People Edge**, simply tap/tick the small circle located on top of this panel.

5. Tap **SELECT CONTACT** and select all the contacts you want by tapping them. Please note that you may need to give access to **People Edge** before it can read your contacts. Tap **DONE** to save the changes. You should now be able to access the selected contacts when you access the Edge panel.

Tap the contacts you want
to add to People Edge

6. To remove a contact from the People Edge, tap the minus icon next to the contact
   you want to remove.

The Bixby

Bixby is a trained virtual assistant that has been built to answer questions and let you interact with your phone in a special way. Bixby is divided into three parts:

1. Bixby Home
2. Bixby Vision
3. Bixby Voice

This section of the guide will show you how to manage Bixby like a pro.

Getting started with Bixby

You would need to setup Bixby when you first start using your device and you would learn how to do that in this section of the guide. To setup this voice assistant:

1. Press the Bixby button (the button next to volume button at the side of the phone).

2. If you see a screen telling you to update Bixby, simply tap **UPDATE** and wait for the update to complete.

3. If you are taken to the home screen after the update, press the Bixby button again to open this virtual assistant.

4. Tap next icon .

5. Read the terms and conditions by tapping the go icon next to each terms and conditions. If you agree to all the terms and conditions, tap **I have read and agreed to all of the above**. Then tap next icon . *If you don't agree to all*

terms/conditions, simply select the one you agree to and click the next icon 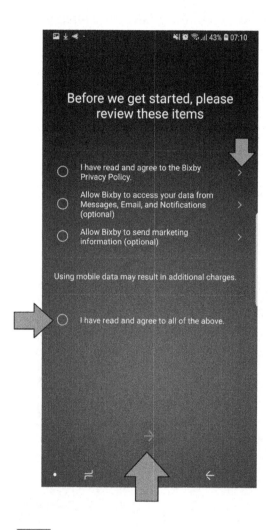.
Please note that you would need to agree to **Bixby Privacy Policy** to continue.

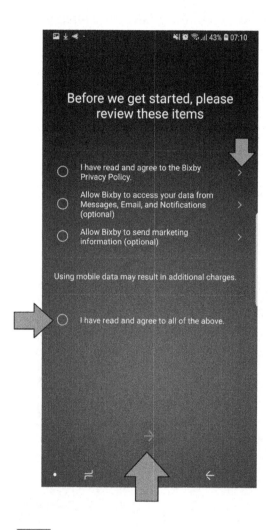

6. Tap the next icon

7. Follow the onscreen instructions to setup and register your voice so that Bixby can recognize your voice.

8. After the voice setup, you would see a screen like the one below. Simply continue to tap **Next** to see all the tips.

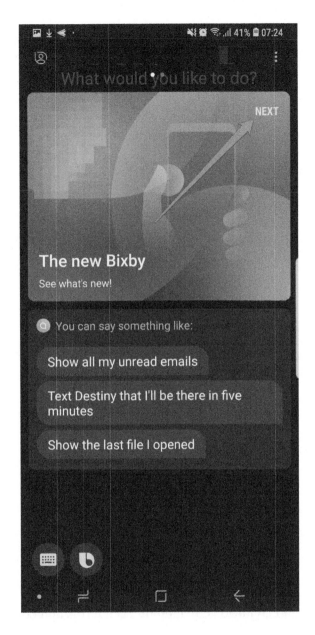

9. When you are done viewing the tips, tap Bixby icon to speak to Bixby. Alternatively, tap the keyboard icon to use a keyboard to ask your question. In addition, you can tap the menu icon ⋮ located at the top of the screen to access options like **settings, quick commands, tutorials** and more.

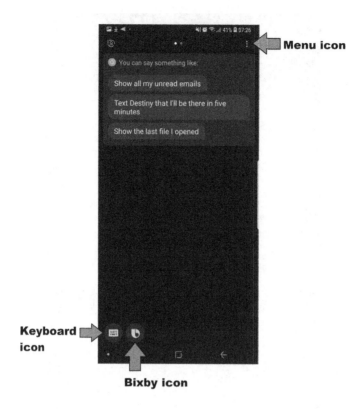

Bixby Home

Bixby Home allows you to access some specific information from your Home screen.

To access and use Bixby Home:

1. Swipe right while on the Home screen and tap **Start**. You might need to swipe more than once before you access Bixby Home.

2. Read the terms and conditions by tapping each terms and conditions. If you agree to all the terms and conditions, tap **I have read and agreed to all of the above**, then tap **Next**. *If you don't agree to all terms/conditions, simply select the one you agree to and click* **Next**. Please note that you would need to agree to **Privacy Policy** and **Terms and Conditions** to continue.

3. To access a card, simply tap the card.

4. To manage a card, tap the menu icon ⋮ next to the card you want to manage. Then tap an option.

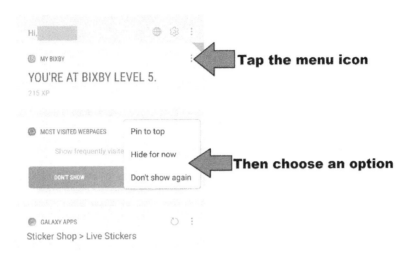

5. To adjust Bixby settings, tap the menu icon ⋮ located at top of the screen and tap **Settings**. Then choose an option.

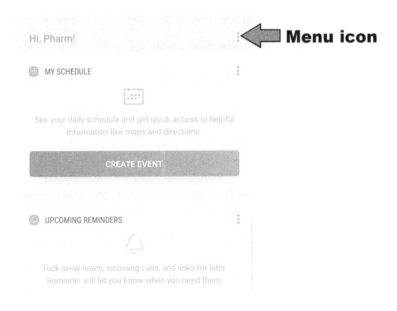

💡 To choose which card is displayed to you on the Bixby home page; while on settings page, tap **Cards**, scroll down and use the status switch to turn off/on a card.

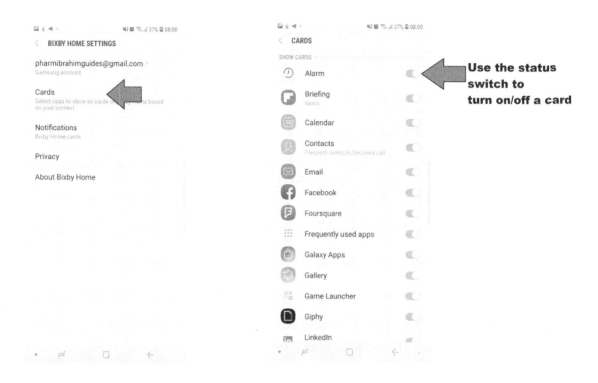

To customize the type of briefing you receive on the Bixby home page, tap the menu icon next to the briefing card and select **Customize content.**

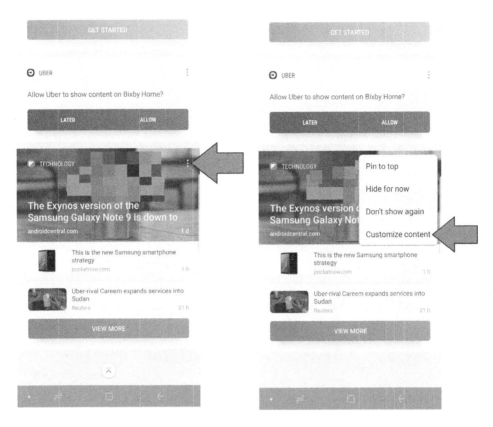

6. Then choose the categories you want to receive information about. Tap the back icon ← to save the changes.

💡 You would see that there are lot of cards in Bixby Home, you could easily narrow down these cards to the one that are important to you. To do this, swipe from left to right on a card to remove it from Bixby Home. Please note that the cards you dismiss using this method would probably appear again after some time. To permanently prevent a card from showing, tap the menu icon ⋮ next to the card and tap **Don't show again**.

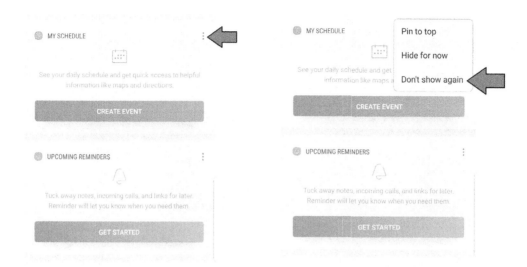

To make the card appear again, tap the menu icon located at the top of the screen, select **Settings**, then select **Cards**. Tap the status switch next to the card you want to show again.

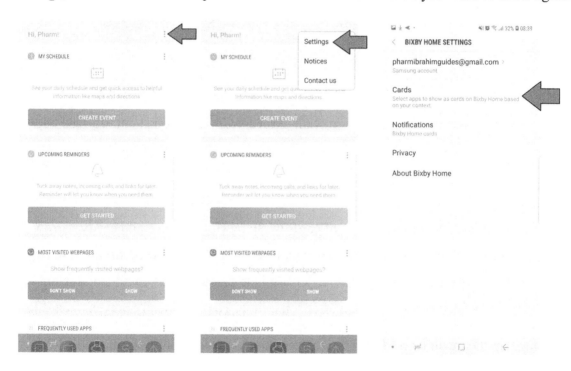

Bixby Voice

Bixby voice allows you to interact with Bixby using your voice.

Speaking to Bixby

One of the ways you would interact with Bixby is by speaking to it. The other way would be to use the keyboard icon .

To get Bixby into action, you would need to get its attention. To do that, perform any of the actions below:

1. Press the Bixby button located next to the volume button at the side of your phone and speak your command while still pressing it.

2. Alternatively, you can get Bixby's attention by saying **Hi Bixby!** However, you may need to enable this feature before you can put it to use. To enable **Hi Bixby** function:

   - Press the dedicated Bixby button once (the button located next to the volume button at the side of the phone).

   - Tap the menu icon located at top of the screen and select **Settings**.

- Tap **Voice wake-up.** Make sure the indicator switch under **Wake with "Hi, Bixby"** is enabled (see the picture below).

- If you want to increase the sensitivity of Bixby to the wake word, drag the slider under **Wake-up sensitivity** to medium or high position.

When Bixby is activated, it will respond by displaying a small action box on the screen. Bixby will then give you an answer.

In addition, occasionally, you may notice that the question you asked Bixby is different from what it types into the action box. What Bixby types into the action box is what it thinks you have said.

💡 You can train Bixby to recognize your voice better. To do this:

1. Press the dedicated Bixby button once (the button located next to the volume button at the side of the phone).

2. Tap the menu icon ⋮ located at the top of the screen and tap **Settings**.

3. Tap **Voice wake-up**.

4. Tap **Improve voice wake-up accuracy** and follow the onscreen instructions.

In addition, you could change the voice of Bixby to a male voice. To do this, repeat steps 1 and 2 above and select **Language and voice style**. Then select **John**.

💡 Usually, you could get example commands when you tap the app icon that appears after giving a command. For example, if you give a calendar-related command, you should see a small calendar app icon after you finish giving the command. Simply tap this icon to see more example commands.

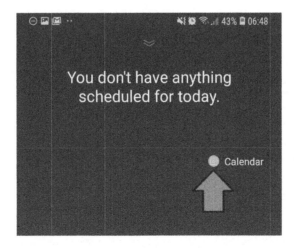

What about Typing?

The interesting thing is that Bixby can also listen when you command it using the on-screen keyboard. You can type in command and get a similar result just as you would get by speaking to it. This is a great feature especially if you can't speak to Bixby for one reason or the other e.g. if you are in a noisy place or your microphone is not working properly.

To use the Bixby typing feature:

5. Press the Bixby button (located next to the volume button).

6. Tap the keyboard icon located at the bottom of the screen

7. Type your command.

- Tap the send icon and wait for a reply. Alternatively, tap **Go** on the on-screen keyboard.

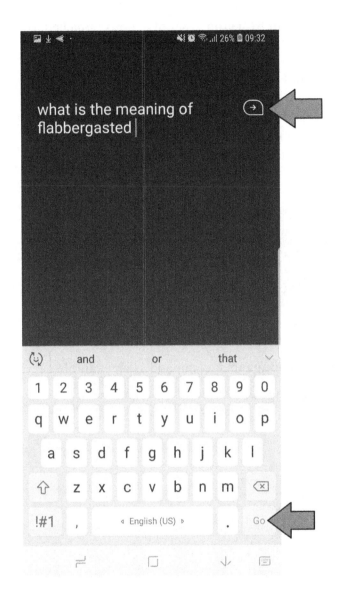

Using Quick Commands to Manage Bixby Like a Pro

Quick commands allow you to use Bixby in a special way. When you say a specific quick command, you trigger a set of actions from Bixby.

Quick Commands include:

a) Good morning b) Going out c) On my way d) Driving etc.

For example, if you say **Good Morning**, a set of actions (attached to Good Morning) are performed by Bixby.

To access quick command menu:

1. Press the dedicated Bixby button once (the button located next to the volume button at the side of the phone).

2. Tap the menu icon ⋮ located at top of the screen and tap **Quick commands**.

3. Then tap a quick command. To see more quick commands, swipe left or right. Let's use **Good morning** quick command as an example.

a) Tap "Good Morning".

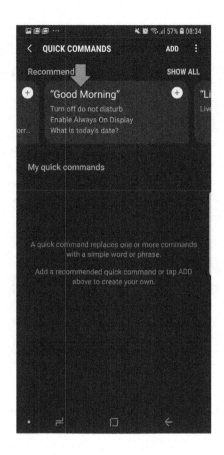

b) Tap **Add a command** to add new command. Then tap on **Select a command**. Tap an app or a category. Then choose example commands from the list.

Alternatively, select **Type a command** or **Say a command** to type or say your command.

c) To delete a command, tap the **X** icon next to the command.

d) To change **Good Morning** to another phrase or statement, tap it and edit the name as you wish.

e) Tap **Save** to save the changes.

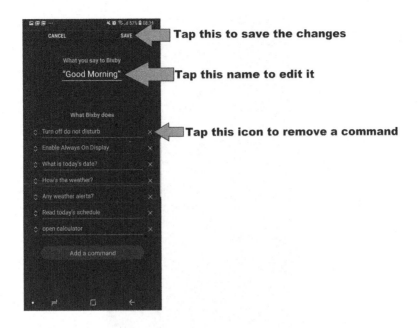

f) After tapping "Save", **Good Morning** should appear under **My quick commands** tab. If it does not appear, tap the plus icon next to Good morning.

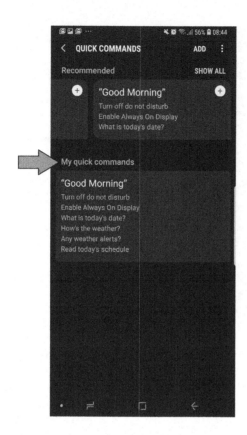

g) To delete a quick command, tap and hold it and select **Delete**.

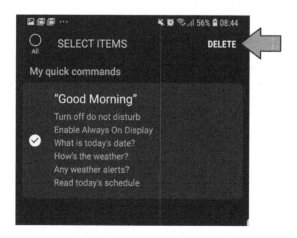

h) To see all quick command, tap **Show All**.

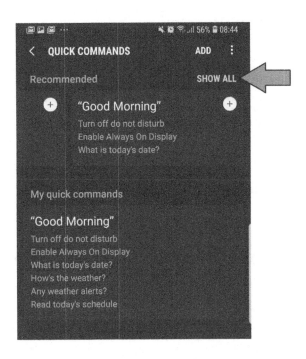

That is all! Now you can get Bixby to perform all the chosen commands by saying **Good Morning**.

You could add more quick commands by tapping **Add** located on the top of the screen. Then follow the prompts.

Using Bixby to Open Apps or Programs

One of those things you would probably want to use Bixby for is accessing your apps. You can quickly open an app by saying **Open**, then mention the name of the app. For example, to open settings, say or type **Open settings.** To open calculator, say **Open calculator**.

You may also say **Launch settings** instead of **Open settings.**

In addition, you may give a more specific command like **Launch Wi-Fi Settings** to open the Wi-Fi settings. To turn off wireless network, say **Turn off wireless network** and so on.

Using Bixby with Notification

To access your notification, simple say **Do I have any notification?**

Using Bixby with Calendar

One of the fantastic features that Bixby can do for you is making an appointment. This personal assistant is built to work with your device Calendar making it easy for it to make appointments.

With just few commands, you can get Bixby to put an event or appointment into your Calendar. **To do this:**

1. Press the Bixby button located next to the volume button at the side of your phone and say your command while still pressing it. Alternatively, say **Hi Bixby!**

2. Say whatever you want to include in the Calendar. For example, you can say any of the following:

- Appointment with Clinton for Monday at 1 p.m.

- Add meeting with Ibrahim at 10 a.m. on Sunday to my calendar.

- Lecture on Friday with my family members at 3 p.m. Please note that you can also say all the examples given above in other ways. The most important thing is to get Bixby to understand what you are saying.

- To edit your events, go to the calendar app. After opening the calendar app, simply tap on the event you want to edit and make any necessary adjustment.

In addition, you can check how your calendar looks. To do this, click the microphone button and say, **"What is on my calendar today?"** or say, **"Any appointment today**?" or just any variant. Note that you can also ask Bixby about your calendar for a day in the future. To do this, say **"Any appointment schedule for tomorrow?"** or say, **"Any appointment on November 1st?"**

In addition, you could cancel an event by saying **Cancel tomorrow's event**. Or say **Cancel today's event.**

In case Bixby sets a wrong appointment, you can edit it in the calendar app using your on-screen keyboard instead of trying to say another word. Editing any misinformation with keyboard appears smarter and faster.

In addition, instead of speaking, you may type any of the commands mentioned above into the search box to get a similar result.

You could get example commands by tapping on the calendar app icon (see the picture below) that usually appears after making a calendar-related commands.

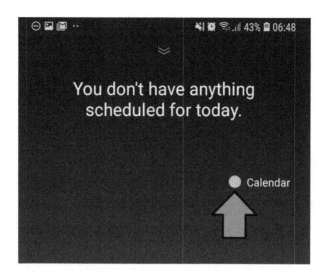

Using Bixby to Set Reminders

There are probably many things going through your mind and it will be quite interesting if you can get a virtual assistant to assist in remembering some of your duties. Fortunately, Bixby can help you in this regard.

To set a reminder using Bixby:

1. Press the Bixby button located next to the volume button at the side of your phone and say your command while still pressing it. Alternatively, say **Hi Bixby!**

2. Say whatever you want to set a reminder for. For example, you can say the following:

   - Remind me to fix the car by 3 p.m.

   - Remind me to drop the bread at the restaurant.

   - Remind me to pick my daughter by 4 p.m.

   - Remind me to call Ibrahim at 1 p.m. and so on.

Please note that it is probably not compulsory that you put **remind** in every statement as I did above. But I would advise that you to do so whenever you can. This is because it will help Bixby to easily get what you are saying and avoid any confusion.

In case Bixby sets a wrong reminder, you can edit it in Reminder app using your on-screen keyboard. In addition, to see all your reminders, simply say **Show me my reminders**. Or say **Show me my reminders for today**.

You could get example commands by tapping on reminder app icon (see the picture below) that usually appears after making a reminder-related commands.

Using Bixby with Alarm and Timer

You can also set an alarm or timer using this virtual assistant.

To do this:

1. Repeat the first step mentioned above.

2. Say the time for alarm. For example, you can say: "**set an alarm for 1 p.m. every Monday**" or "**alarm for 1 p.m. every Wednesday**" or "**set an everyday alarm for 2 p.m.**" or "**set an alarm for 1 p.m. on 24th of October**".

3. To set a timer, you might say **Set a timer for 15 minutes**.

4. When it has grabbed the information, the alarm would appear and it will tell you that it has set the alarm.

5. To cancel an alarm, you might say **Cancel my alarm** or **Say turn off all my alarms**.

You could get example commands by tapping on Alarm and Timer app icon (see the picture below) that usually appears after making an alarm or timer related commands.

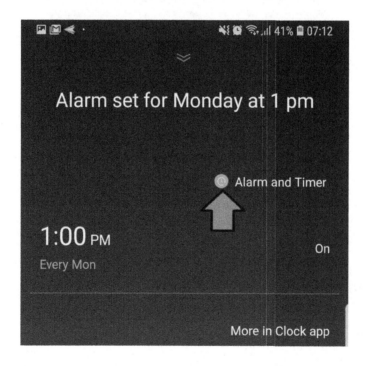

Using Bixby with Clock

You can ask Bixby what your local time is. In addition, it can also tell you the time in a specific place.

1. Say **Hi Bixby!**

2. Then say, "**What is the time?**" or say, "**What is the time in Seattle?**"

Using Bixby to Get Flight Information

You can also use this virtual assistant to get information about a flight. This is a smarter way to know when an airplane will take off.

For example, you can say **Flight status of Delta 400** to get the information about this flight.

Using Bixby with Weather App

To know about the weather condition of a place, just say "**What's the weather going to be like today?**". You may also know about the weather condition of a place by asking "**What is the weather condition of New York today?**"

Using Bixby with Mail App

You can instruct Bixby to compose an email for you. To do this:

1. Press the Bixby button located next to the volume button at the side of your phone and speak your command while still pressing it. Alternatively, say **Hi Bixby!**

2. Then give the command. For example, you can say:

- Send an email to Clinton.

- Send an email to Clinton and Steve.

- Search for emails from Pharm Ibrahim.

- Show all the emails I received today.

- Show me my unread emails.

- Read all the emails marked as important.

- Search for emails from Steve and mark them as important.

Please note that you will usually have to include one or more information before you send the email. Simply follow the voice prompts to add subject and email body.

You could get example commands by tapping on the email app icon (see the picture below) that usually appears after making email-related commands.

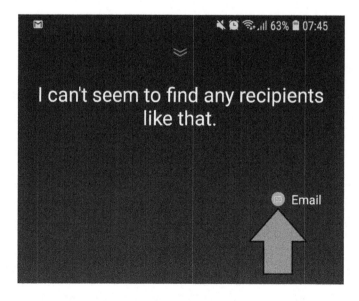

Using Bixby with Map App

You can also use the Bixby to search the map. This virtual assistant is built to work with the Map app on your device. **To get how the map of a place looks like**:

1. Repeat the first step above.

2. Then say the map of an area you want to get. For example, you may say:

    - Map of Seattle.

    - Show me the map of Seattle.

What about Math?

Bixby can also help you with some mathematical calculations and conversions. For example, you can tell Bixby **What is the square root of four?** You can also say **convert one meter to centimeter** or **convert 1 ton to grams**.

Using Bixby to Get Definitions

Also, you can ask Bixby for meaning of words. For example, you may say **what is the meaning of flabbergasted?**

Bixby Voice Settings

The settings tab allows you to manage Bixby's functions. To access Bixby's settings:

1. Press the dedicated Bixby button once (the button located next to the volume button at the side of the phone).

2. Tap the menu icon ⋮ located at top of the screen and tap **Settings**.

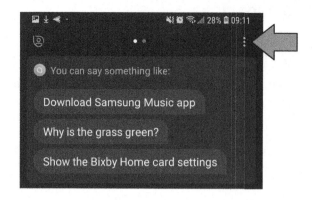

3. Tap an option.

The settings menu allows you to manage Bixby better. I would advise that you take time to go through the various settings options on the settings page.

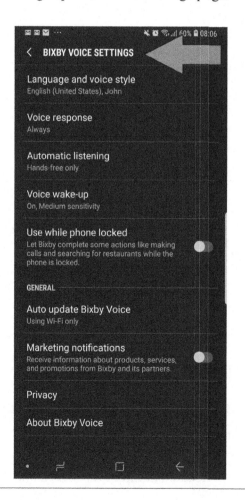

How to Control Your Privacy When Using Bixby Voice

To control how Bixby manages/accesses your information:

4. Press the dedicated Bixby button once (the button located next to the volume button at the side of the phone).

5. Tap the menu icon ⋮ located at the topmost part of the screen and tap **Settings**.

6. Tap **Privacy.**

7. Tap an option to disable or enable.

Troubleshooting Bixby

Although much efforts have been put into making this virtual assistant, I am quite sure that Bixby will misbehave at one time or the other. When this happens, there are few things to do.

- **Ensure that you are connected to a strong network**: If you have a bad or no internet connection, Bixby may not work properly. Therefore, the first thing to check when Bixby starts to misbehave is the internet connection.

- **Use the Virtual Keyboard**: You may need to use the keyboard to pass your message to Bixby if you find out that it is not getting your speech. Many of what you say (If not all) can also be typed into the Bixby's search bar. Please go to page 206 to learn more about this.

- **Close the Bixby Voice app and press the Bixby button to access it again**.

- **Try to Restart Your Phone**: If you find out that methods mentioned above do not work, try restarting your phone.

Conclusion

Bixby is like a learning machine and it is being improved upon. If you are having difficulty passing your message across to it, you may try typing some of your commands into the command box. I strongly believe you will know how to use it more as time goes on.

Bixby Vision

Bixby Vision allows you to interact with images in an educating manner. It also gives you more understanding of what you are looking at. When first using Bixby Vision, you may need to agree to some terms and conditions.

To Use Bixby Vision:

1. Launch the camera app of your phone.
2. Aim the lens of the camera at what you want to capture.
3. Tap the Bixby button. You can use the Bixby Vision to extract texts, translate a language, scan Barcodes etc. If you are using Bixby Vision for the first time, simply follow the on-screen instructions to set it up. Please note that you would need to agree to terms and conditions when setting up Bixby Vision. To do this, scroll down to read all the terms/conditions and agree as appropriate.

Bixby Vision Icon

An alternate way to access Bixby Vision is tapping on Bixby Vision icon ⬡ located on the applications screen.

4. Choose an option. For example, if you are trying to extract a text, scroll right or left and tap **Text**. Then tap **Text** again to extract the texts.

5. To manage Bixby Vision settings, tap the menu icon ⋮ (see the picture above) and select **Settings**.

6. To exit, tap the back button ← .

You can also access Bixby vision while using the Gallery app. Simply launch the **Gallery** app, tap an image and tap the Bixby button. Please note that some pictures may not have Bixby button.

Using the Web

Internet App

Opening the Internet Browser

The first thing you would need to do to use the Internet app is to open it. To do this:

1. From the Home screen, tap **Internet** .

2. Alternatively, go to the app screen by swiping up from the bottom of the screen and tap **Samsung** folder. Tap **Internet** .

3. If you are using the Internet app for the first time, follow the prompts to get started.

Get to Know the Internet Browser Interface

When you open the Internet app, you should see the following buttons/icons:

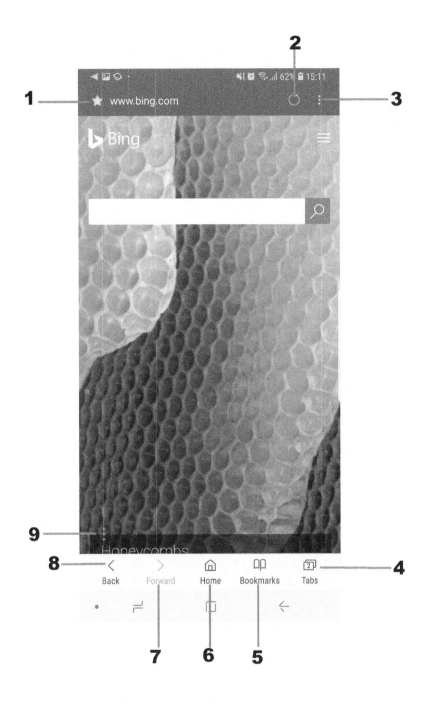

1	**Favorite: Tap this icon to bookmark a webpage.**
2	**Refresh:** Tapping this icon reloads a webpage.
3	**Menu icon:** Tap this icon to access additional options such as **Find on page** and **save**

	webpage etc.
4	**Tabs:** Tap this to navigate between different webpages. Tap and hold the tab icon to quickly open your browser's home page.
5	**Bookmarks:** Tap this icon to access bookmark pages, saved pages and history.
6	**Home:** Tap this icon to go to the browser's Home page. To quickly change the default Home page, tap and hold the Home icon [home icon] and select **Other.** Then enter the website of your choice and tap **OK.**
7	**Forward**: Tap this icon to return to the page you just left.
8	**Back:** Tap this icon to revisit the page you just visited. To quickly access browsing history, tap and hold the back button [back arrow icon]
9	**Quick Menu:** Tap this button [menu icon] to access the quick menu. Quick menu allows you to quickly share a webpage, increase webpage font, or open a new tab. To move this icon to another location, simply tap, hold and drag the icon to the new location. To remove the icon; tap, hold and drag it to the top of the screen (where remove icon [remove icon] is located). To manage Quick menu options, tap the menu icon [menu icon] (located next to address bar) and select **Extensions**. Then tap **Quick menu** and select an option.

Customizing the Home Page

The Home page is the page that opens when you open your Internet browser app. Fortunately, you can choose what appears on your Internet Home page.

To do this:

- While the Internet browser is opened, tap the menu icon 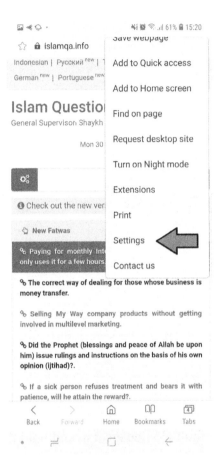, then scroll down and tap on **Settings.**

- Tap **Home page** and choose an option.

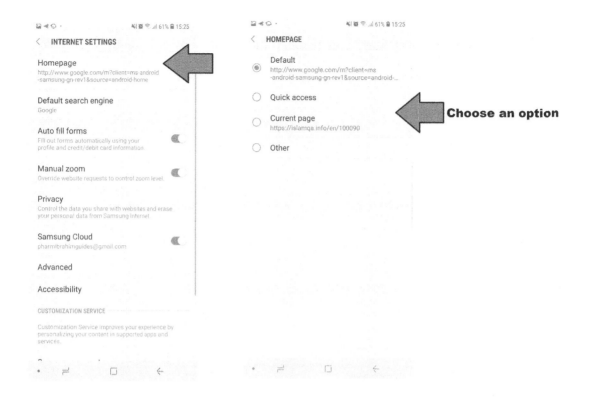

- To go to the Home page while using your internet browser, tap the internet browser Home button 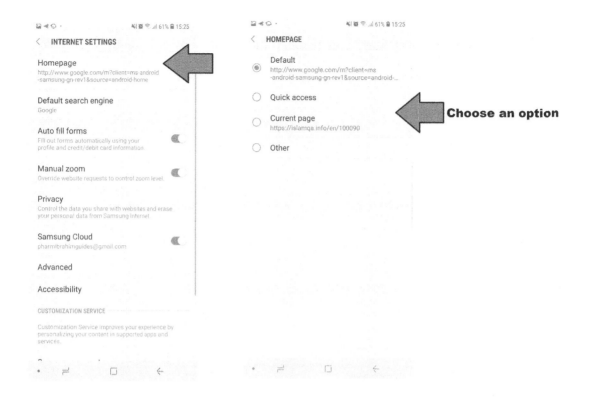 .

To quickly change the default Homepage, tap and hold the Home icon 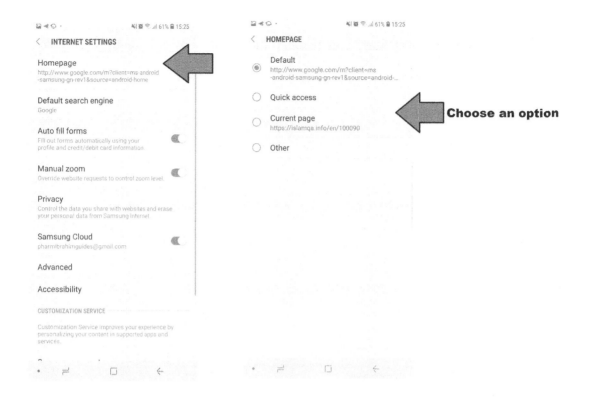 and select an option.

Using the Address/Search Bar

Every web browser must have an address bar and Internet browser also has one. This bar serves the function of URL address bar and search bar. By default, the searches done on this bar is executed by Google. To learn how to change the search engine to another one, please go to page 242.

You choose whether to launch a webpage or search for a term based on what you type into the address bar. For example, if you type **Freedom to** into the address bar and tap **Go**, Google search results for that phrase is displayed. On the other hand, if you type **Freedom.to** and tap **Go**, you will be taken to the website bearing the name.

Internet browser makes website suggestions to you based on the sites you have recently visited, to choose any of this suggested site, tap it.

When you begin to type inside the address bar, Internet browser automatically makes suggestions beneath your typing. You can choose any of these suggestions to make things faster.

Zooming a Webpage in Internet Browser

To zoom in a webpage in Internet browser, place two fingers on the webpage and spread them apart. To zoom out, place two fingers on the webpage and move them closer. To force zoom a webpage that doesn't readily respond to a zoom request, turn on the **Manual zoom.** To do this, while the Internet browser is opened, tap the menu icon ⋮ located at the top of the screen, then scroll down and tap on **Settings**. Tap the status switch next to **Manual Zoom.**

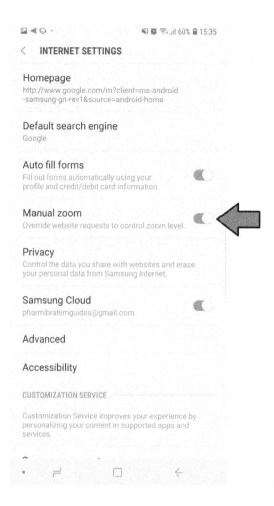

Using Tabs on Internet Browser

The tabs allow you to open different webpages at once. You can open many tabs at once on Internet browser.

To manage browsing tabs:

1. Tap the tab icon ⬜ located at the bottom of the screen.
2. To open a new tab, tap **New Tab**.

3. To access a tab you have opened before, tap the tab icon and tap your desired tab.

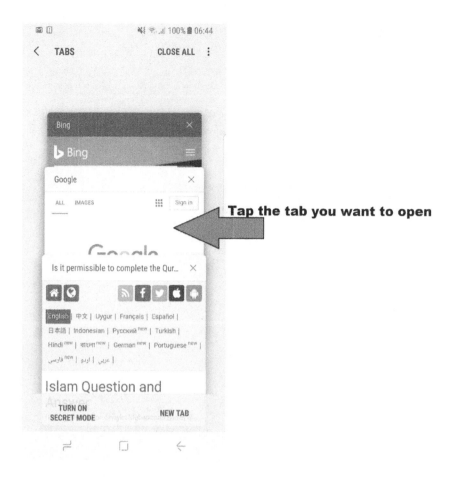

Tap the tab you want to open

4. To close a tab, tap the **X** icon at the top right corner of the thumbnail of the tab you want to close.

5. To close all tabs, while on the tabs' screen, tap **CLOSE ALL** located at the top of the screen.

You can quickly move from one tab to another. To do this, simply swipe left/right on the address bar.

Swipe Left or right on the address bar to move to another tab.

Block distractions.
Focus on what matters.

We believe that productivity means prioritizing the things that truly matter. Freedom helps protect your time and attention from online distractions on your Mac, Windows, and iOS devices so that you can do more of what you love.

Favorites (Bookmarks)

With several billions of webpages in the internet world, you just have to select your favorites. Just like other modern day browsers, Internet browser gives you the opportunity to select a favorite or bookmark a page. This makes it easier to visit the website or webpage in the future.

To bookmark a webpage:

1. Open the website you want to bookmark.

2. Tap the menu icon ⋮ located at the top of the screen and select **Add to Bookmarks**.

3. Key in the **Title** you want.

4. Tap **Save.**

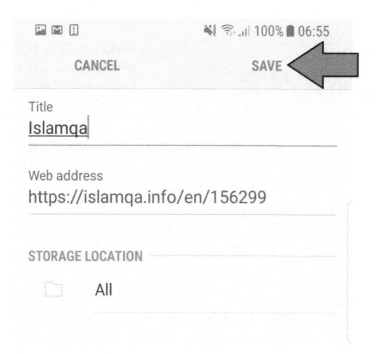

5. By default, your bookmarks would be stored under **All** folder. To save a bookmark in a new folder:

    a) Repeat steps 1 and 2 above.

    b) Tap **All**, then tap **Create**.

    c) Enter a name and tap **Save**.

    d) Then tap this newly created folder to select it.

e) Thereafter, enter a name for your bookmark and tap **Save.**

To quickly add a bookmark, just open the webpage and tap favorite icon next to the address bar.

Accessing Your Bookmarks/Favorites

After you have added a webpage to your favorite list, you would need to access this list sooner or later. To access your bookmarks, tap the Bookmark icon ![bookmark] (located at the bottom of the screen). If you can't see this bookmark icon, swipe down from the middle part of the screen to bring it into view.

Saving a Webpage

Webpages contain a lot of information and you would probably need to schedule some webpages for later reading. Saving a webpage is a great way to do this. When you find an interesting information online and you don't have the time to read it, you can save it for a later reading.

To save a webpage, open the webpage and tap ⋮ (next to address bar), then select **Save webpage**.

Accessing Your Saved Pages

After you have saved a page, you would need to access this page sooner or later. To do this, tap the **Bookmarks** icon (located at the bottom of the screen) and tap **Saved Pages** located at the top of the screen. To delete a saved page, tap and hold the page you want to delete and select **Delete**.

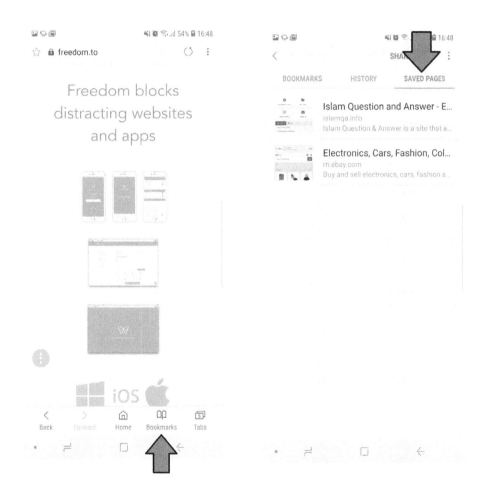

Changing the Search Engine

The default search engine on Internet browser is Google. Some people may love to change this to another search engine.

You can change the Internet browser Search Engine by following the steps highlighted below:

1. While the browser is opened, tap the menu icon ⋮ (next to address bar) and select **Settings**.

2. Tap on **Default search engine** and select a search engine.

Making Internet App Your Default Browser

If you have multiple browsers on your device, you can make Internet app your default browser. To do this:

1. Swipe down from the top of the screen and select the settings icon .

2. Tap **Apps** and tap the menu icon ⋮ .
3. Tap **Default apps**.
4. Tap **Browser app** and choose **Samsung Internet**.

💡 You can use the method mentioned above to set other favorite app(s) as default app(s). For example, if you have many messaging apps on your device, you can select a default messaging app using this method.

Managing the History List

If the secret mode is not enabled, Internet browser collects the history of the webpages you visit and stores them.

To access your history:

1. Tap the **Bookmarks** 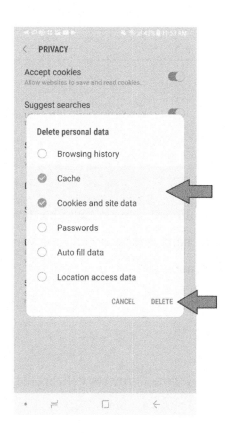 (located at the bottom of the screen).

2. Tap **History**.

To clear the browsing data, tap ⋮ (located at the top of the screen) > **Settings** > **Privacy** > **Delete personal data.** Select what you would like to delete and tap **Delete.**

In addition, if you see that a website/webpage is misbehaving, you can try deleting the *cache, cookies and site data* and see if this would solve the problem. To do this, tap

⋮ (located at the top of the screen) > **Settings** > **Privacy** > **Delete personal data.** Select **Cache, Cookies and site data** and tap **Delete.**

Sharing a Webpage with Friends

To share a webpage with friends, open the Internet app and tap the menu icon ⋮ next to the address bar. Tap on **Share**. Then choose an app and follow the prompts.

Add Your Favorite Webpage to the Home Screen

You can make your favorite webpage a shortcut on the Home screen. This allows you to easily access the webpage directly from your Home screen. To do this:

1. Open a webpage and tap on the menu icon ⋮ (next to the address bar).
2. Tap **Add to Home screen**.

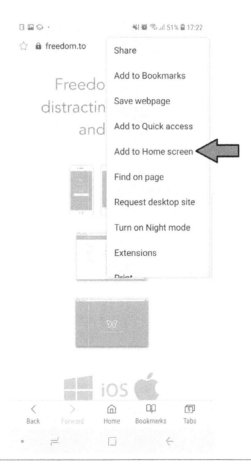

3. Tap **Add.**

4. To see the newly added webpage, tap the home button ⬜ (located at the bottom of the screen). If you can't see it on the first Home screen, swipe left to check another Home screen.

Printing Web Pages on the Internet browser

Printing on the Internet browser is quite fantastic. You can initiate the printing process by tapping on the menu icon ⋮ (next to the address bar). Then tap **Print.** Tap the **dropdown arrow** to select a printer and follow the prompts. To adjust the printing options, tap **Copies**.

To save the webpage as a pdf, tap the dropdown arrow and select **Save as PDF.**

Thereafter, tap the yellow **PDF** icon and choose a folder. Then tap **Done** to download.

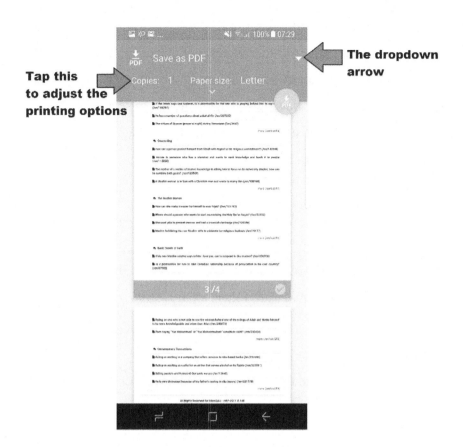

Tap this to adjust the printing options

The dropdown arrow

Secret Mode

There are times when you will not want your browser to save any information about your visit to a webpage. For instance, if you don't want a website to save cookies on your device or you don't want your children to know you are browsing about favorite gifts to buy for them.

In addition, secret mode browsing allows for multiple sessions. For example, you may access your Yahoo mail account (or another web account) on a normal window and use the secret mode tab to open the Yahoo mail account of that of your friend or family member without logging out of your account. Pages viewed in secret mode are not listed in your browser history or search history and leave no traces (such as cookies) on your device.

To activate the Secret mode, in the toolbar at the bottom of the screen, tap **Tabs** → **Turn on Secret mode.**

Then tap **Set password** to protect your secret mode data with a password. You may also tap **Do not use password** if you don't want to use a password.

To deactivate the Secret mode, close the Internet app. Alternatively, tap the tab button , tap **Close All** (located at the top of the screen) and select **Turn Off Secret Mode**.

More on Internet browser Settings

Many options under settings have already been discussed, but there are still some that I would like to mention.

1. **Auto fill profile:** Use this option to enable Internet browser to save your form entries whenever you fill in information into an online form so that it can be used when you are filling similar forms in the future.

2. **Privacy**: Use this option to access settings such as **cookies**, **personal data** and so on. You can use the privacy tab to delete history information on your browser. To do this, tap **Delete personal data**.

3. **Advanced**: Use this option to access advanced options like **JavaScript**, **Pop-up blocker**, **Status bar**, **Manage website data**, **Web text size** and **Web**

notifications. In addition, you could use the option **Save content to** under the Advanced tab to determine where contents from internet are stored to.

4. **Accessibility**: You can manage *high contrast mode* under this tab.

5. **Samsung account**: This tab displays the Samsung account address on your mobile phone.

6. **Personal information**: Use this tab to manage the information that can be sent to Samsung in order to provide you a customized experience.

7. **About Samsung Internet:** Use this option to get software information about the Internet app.

Samsung Pass

Samsung Pass allows you to easily login into websites by storing login information for you. You would need to set up biometrics to use Samsung Pass. You can use Samsung Pass to autofill your username and password.

To use Samsung Pass:

1. Swipe down from the top of the screen and tap the **settings icon** .
2. Tap **Biometrics and Security**.
3. Scroll down and tap **Samsung Pass**.
4. Carefully follow the on-screen information to set up this feature.

Thereafter, make sure the autofill option is set to use Samsung Pass. To do this:

1. Swipe down from the top of the screen and tap the settings icon .

2. Tap the search bar located at the top of the screen and type in **Autofill** into the search bar. The result filters as you type. In the search result, select **Autofill service**. Then make sure that **Autofill with Samsung Pass** is selected.

That is all. The next time you sign in to a website or service in Samsung Internet or sign in to an app, you would be prompted to save your username and password in Samsung Pass. Simply select **Save** when prompted.

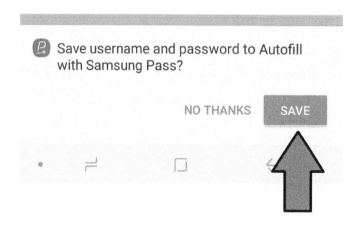

More on the Menu Icon

Many options under the **menu** tab ⋮ have already been discussed, but I would still like to point out few more things.

1. **Add to Quick access**: Use this option to add a webpage to your quick access list so that you can access it easily in the future from the Internet app Home page. To make sure you go to Quick access page when you tap the Internet browser home button 🏠 , tap and hold Internet browser home button 🏠 and select Quick access.

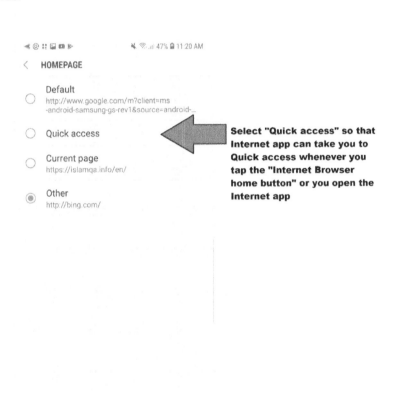

2. **Add to Home screen:** Use this option to make a webpage a shortcut on your Home screen.

3. **Find on page:** Use this option to search for a word or a phrase on a webpage.

4. **Request desktop site:** Use this option to request the desktop version of a webpage.

5. **Turn on Night mode:** Use this option to give a webpage a darkish background.

6. **Extensions:** This allows you to do more when using the Internet app. To see which extensions are available on Internet app, tap **Extensions.**

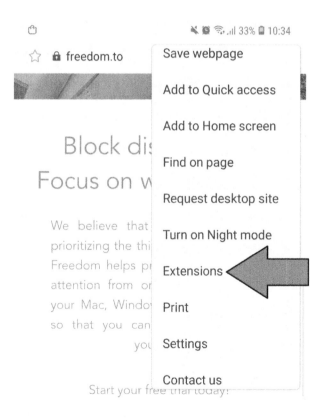

Troubleshooting the Internet browser

Internet browser may sometimes refuse to work properly, or it may hang. If this happens, just close the browser and open it again. To close the Internet app, tap the recent button (located at the bottom of the screen) to view all the opened apps and tap **X** next to the Internet app thumbnail. If the browser refuses to close, try restarting your phone.

Recent Button

In addition, if you see that a website/webpage is misbehaving, you can try deleting the *cache, cookies and site data* and see if this would solve the problem. To do this, tap

Internet app menu icon ⋮ (located at the top of the screen) > **Settings** > **Privacy** > **Delete personal data.** Select **Cache, Cookies and site data** and tap **Delete**.

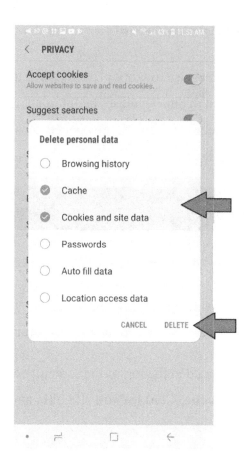

Troubleshooting Internet Connection when Using the Internet Browser

Internet browser may sometimes refuse to browse the internet. When this happens, you may try any of the suggestions below:

1. Check if you are connected to a wireless network. When Wi-Fi is connected, active and it is communicating with a wireless Access Point, **Wi-Fi active icon** is displayed on the status bar at the top of the screen. If your phone is not connected to a network, swipe down from the top of the screen and tap the settings icon

    > **Connections**. Tap **Wi-Fi** and tap On/Off to turn Wi-Fi on.

Wi-Fi Active Icon

2. If you are trying to use a cellular connection and not a Wi-Fi connection, then check your cellular data connection. Swipe down from the top of the screen, tap the settings icon ✿ > **Connections** >**Data Usage**. Then make sure the switch next to **Mobile data** is turned on.

3. If you are trying to roam while abroad, check that you have allowed roaming. Swipe down from the top of the screen and tap the **settings icon** ✿ > **Connections** > **Mobile networks** > **Data Roaming**. Then make sure the switch next to **Data Roaming** is switched on. Please note that when roaming, international roaming charges may apply.

If you can't still browse after trying all the options above, then make sure that you have not mistakenly/knowingly installed a new browsing setting on your phone. If you have installed new settings from a text message, then uninstall the new settings. To do this, swipe down from the top of the screen and tap the settings icon ✿ > **Apps**. Look for the new settings. Tap the new settings and tap **Uninstall**.

Communication

Calling

Learn how to use the calling functions, such as making and answering calls, using options available during a call and using call-related features.

Making, Answering, Rejecting and Silencing a Call

To make a call or silence a call:

1. While on the Home screen, tap **Phone** and enter a phone number. If the keypad does not appear on the screen, tap the keypad button to show the keypad. To call a number on your contact, tap the **Contact** button on the Phone app screen.

2. To make a call from the **Recents** tab, tap the **Recents** tab located at the top of the screen.

3. To make a phone call, tap a contact and tap the phone icon .

Tap the contact you want to call

Call icon

4. To silence or reduce the volume of an incoming call, press the volume down button (located at the side of the phone).

💡 You can access apps/items on your phone while receiving a call. To do this, tap the home key ⬜ located at the lower side of the screen and tap the item/app you want to access.

💡 To call the contact whose message or contact details are currently on the screen, bring the phone close to your ear. However, please note that you may need to enable this option. To do this, swipe down from the top of the screen and tap the **settings icon** ⚙ > **Advanced features.** Then tap the status switch next to **Direct call**.

To answer a call or reject an incoming call:

1. To receive an incoming call, tap or drag the **Green phone icon** .

2. To decline an incoming call, tap or drag the **Red phone icon** .

3. To reply with a text, swipe up from the bottom of the screen or tap **Send Message**.

4. Then tap one of the pre-written messages. Alternatively, tap **Compose new message** and write your message.

Choose a message from the list or tap on "Compose new message" to reply with a message of your choice

If you are using an app, a pop-up screen is displayed for the incoming call, just tap the corresponding icon to accept, decline the call or reply with a message.

In addition, you can create rejection messages of your own. From the Home screen, tap

Phone > Menu icon ⋮ > Settings > Quick decline message , enter a message and tap **Plus icon +.** To delete a message, tap the minus icon next to it.

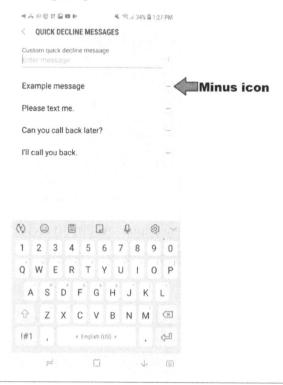

Minus icon

If a phone number calls you or you call a number and you don't have it on your contact list, you can easily add it to your contact list. To do this, tap **Phone** app and tap **Recents.** Then tap the contact and tap **Details.** Tap **Create Contact** (located at the bottom of the screen) and follow the prompts.

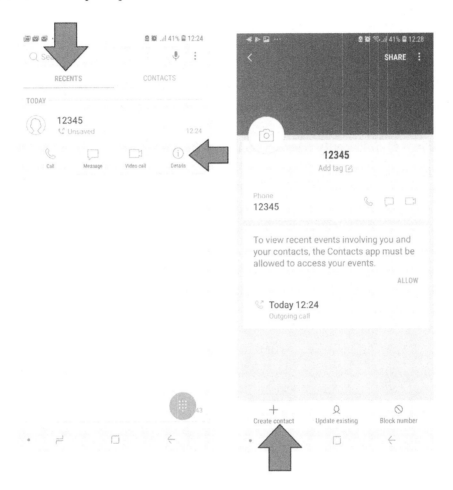

To quickly reject an incoming call with a preset rejection message, place your finger on the heart rate sensor for two seconds while the phone screen is facing down. The heart rate sensor/monitor is located next to the flash light at the back of your phone. *Please note that this option may only work when your device is turned over and the screen is off. In addition, you might need to enable this feature.*

To enable quick reply and edit the preset rejection message:

1. Swipe down from the top of the screen and select the settings icon . Tap **Display** tab.

2. Scroll down and tap **Edge Screen**.

3. Tap **Edge Lighting**.

4. Tap the menu icon located at the top of the screen.

5. Tap **Quick reply**.

6. To enable this feature, tap the status switch next to **Off**.

7. Type in a **Quick Reply Message** and tap the back icon next to QUICK REPLY to save the changes.

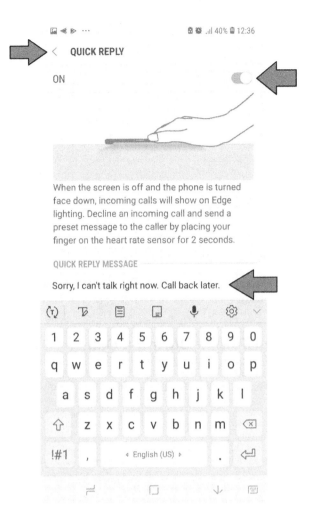

ON

When the screen is off and the phone is turned face down, incoming calls will show on Edge lighting. Decline an incoming call and send a preset message to the caller by placing your finger on the heart rate sensor for 2 seconds.

QUICK REPLY MESSAGE

Sorry, I can't talk right now. Call back later.

Changing the Ringing Tone

If you don't like the default ringtone, you could change it to another one. To do this:

1. Swipe down from the top of the screen and select settings icon ⚙. Tap **Sounds and Vibration** tab.
2. Tap **Ringtone**.
3. If needed, select a SIM.
4. If you don't what any sound, scroll up (if needed) and select **Silent**. Alternatively, if you want a very simple sound, select Beep Once.

5. To add your our alert type, tap **Add** located at the top of the screen and follow the prompts.

To change the notification sound on your phone, repeat step 1 above and tap **Notification sounds**. Select a SIM (if needed) and choose an appropriate sound.

Learn How to Use Your Phone During a Call

You can perform any of these tasks when on a call:

Number	Function
1.	Tap the **Menu icon** to hold a current call, view or add a contact or send a message.
2.	Tap the Bluetooth icon to connect to a Bluetooth headset while on a call.
3.	Tap the keypad icon to access the keypad. To hide the keypad, tap the **Hide** icon ▦.
4.	Tap the red phone icon to **end a call**.

5.	Tap this icon to mute the microphone.
6.	To turn speaker on or off, tap the speaker icon.
7.	Tap the plus icon to add another contact to a call or start another call.
8.	Tap extra volume icon to add extra volume to a call.
9.	Call time

To access the application screen while on a call, tap the Home button. If you want to return to the call screen, swipe down from the top of the screen and tap the current call.

Place a New Call While on a Call (Conference Calling)

If your network service provider supports this feature, you can make another call while a call is in progress.

1. From the active call screen, tap **+ Add call**.

2. Dial the new number and tap ![phone icon] **Dial**. When the call is answered:

   i. Tap ![swap icon] **Swap** to switch between the two calls.

   ii. Tap ![merge icon] **Merge** to turn the calls to a conference call.

3. To end a call while on a conference call, tap the dropdown arrow (next to **Conference call**) and select **Drop** next to the call you want to end.

Emergency Calling

You can use Samsung Galaxy Note 9 to make an emergency call. From the Home screen, tap **Phone** icon and enter the emergency telephone number. Note that if you dial 911 in the U.S, your location details may be provided to an emergency service provider even if your settings does not support this.

Please note that an emergency number can be dialed even if the phone is locked.

Using Call Waiting

Call waiting allows you to get another call while you're already in one.

1. To answer the new call, tap or drag **Answer** to the right direction and choose an option:

    i. **Put ...on hold** to place the previous caller on hold while you answer the new call.

    ii. **End call with...** to end the previous call and answer the new call.

2. Once the other call is answered, tap the swap icon next to the contact or phone number you wish to continue talking to. The other(s) would be put on hold.

    To merge the calls, tap the merge icon .

Please note that call waiting may be disabled by default. To enable this feature, tap **Phone** > **Menu icon** ⋮ > **Settings** > **More settings** and tap the switch next to **Call waiting**.

Using the Speed Dial Options

The speed dial allows you to quickly access a number on your contact list. To set up a speed dial:

1. Tap the phone icon .
2. Tap **Contacts** located at the top of the screen.
3. Tap **menu icon** ⋮ located at the top of the screen.
4. Tap **Speed dial numbers**.

5. To add a contact to the speed dial, tap the contact icon ⃝ .

6. To change the speed dial number, tap the dropdown arrow and pick a number. Number one is reserved for voicemail.

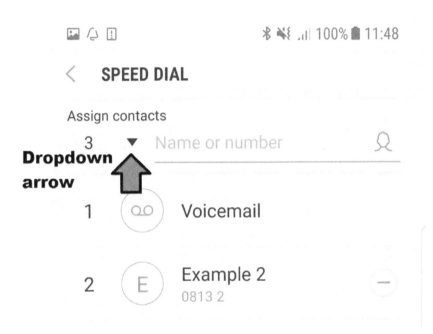

7. To call a contact you have added, tap the phone app icon 📞 and from the dial pad, press and hold the number assigned to the desired contact. To call a contact assigned to a two-digit speed dial, dial the first number, then press and hold the 2nd number.

8. To delete a speed dial number, tap the **Minus (-)** icon next to the assigned contact. Removing a contact from a speed dial list will not delete it from your phone.

Using the Fixed Dialing Option

If you want to select the numbers your mobile phone can call, you need to turn on the fixed dialing. Once done, you can only call the selected numbers and emergency numbers.

1. From the Home screen, tap **Phone app icon** .

2. Tap **menu icon** located at the top of the screen.

3. Tap **Settings**.

4. Scroll down and tap **More settings**.

5. Tap **Fixed Dialing Numbers**.

6. To turn the fixed dialing on, tap **Turn on FDN**, type in your **PIN2** and tap **OK**. Please contact your local network service provider for your PIN2.

7. To turn the fixed dialing off, tap **Turn off FDN**, enter your **PIN2** and tap **OK**.

I am not sure if all network providers support this feature. If you notice that this feature is not available on your phone or it is not working properly, you may need to contact your service provider to know if you can use this feature.

Adding Fixed Dialing Numbers

1. Repeat steps 1 to 5 above.

2. Tap **FDN List**.

3. Tap **ADD** located at the top of the screen.

4. Tap **Name** and enter the required name.

5. Tap **Number** and enter the required phone number.

6. Tap **PIN2** and enter the PIN2. Please contact your local network service provider for your PIN2.

7. To import contacts, tap the menu icon and select **Import from contacts**.

8. Tap **SAVE** located at the top of the screen.

Please note that when FDN is enabled, you may not be able to call any other numbers apart from the numbers on the FDN list and the emergency numbers.

Call Forwarding (Diverting Calls to Another Number)

When you are busy, you can forward incoming calls to another phone number. Please note that your network provider would need to support this feature for it to be available.

1. From the Home screen, tap **Phone app icon** .
2. Tap **menu icon** located at the top of the screen.
3. Tap **Settings**.
4. Scroll down and tap **More settings**.
5. Tap **Call forwarding**.
6. Select **Voice call** or **Video call**.
7. Tap the required divert type and follow the on-screen instructions. For example, to forward all your calls, tap **Always forward**.
8. To turn off call forwarding, select a divert type and select **turn off.**

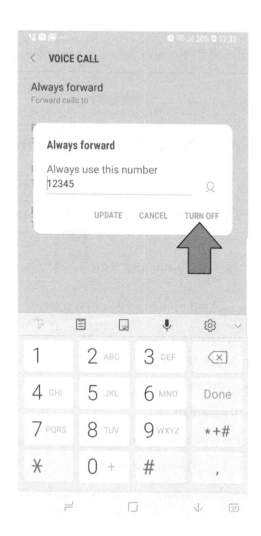

When the call forwarding option is enabled, you should see the call forwarding icon (see the picture below) on the notification bar at the top of the screen.

In addition, depending on your network provider, you may be able to forward calls to your voice mail and listen to them later. To know how to do this, contact your network service provider.

Block Calls

If your service provider supports this feature, you may be able to avoid receiving calls from certain numbers. Please note that the call blocking feature may not affect phone calls made or received via apps (e.g. Skype) installed on your device.

Please note that features available under Call blocking may differ from one service provider to another.

1. From the Home screen, tap **Phone app icon** .

2. Tap **menu icon** located at the top of the screen.

3. Tap **Settings**.

4. Tap **Block numbers**.

5. To add a number to your block list, enter the desired phone number in the **Add phone number** field, then tap the + icon. To add a number from your contacts, tap

   Contacts icon and tap **Done** after adding a contact.

6. To remove a number from your block list, tap the Minus (-) icon next to a name or number on your block list.

7. To make sure that only the numbers that you have their contacts can call you, tap the status switch next to **Block unknown callers**.

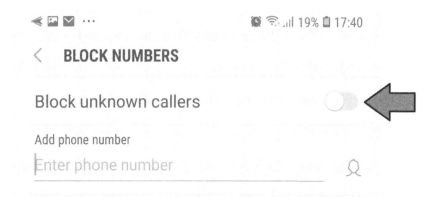

In certain instances, blocking anonymous call may be unbeneficial and even dangerous. For example, blocking anonymous calls may prevent you from accepting calls from those who have something important to tell you (unless you have their contacts). *In addition, if you are not able to use call blocking option after following the instructions above, please contact your network service provider.*

To block a number from call log, follow these steps:

1. From the Home screen, tap **Phone app icon** .

2. Tap **Recents** (located at the top of the screen).

3. Tap **Block number** located at the bottom of the screen.

4. If you have the number you want to block on your contact list, tap **menu icon** located at the top of the screen. Then select **Block contact**.

What about Caller ID?

If your service provider supports this feature, you may prevent your service provider from displaying your number(ID) when you call another person.

1. From the Home screen, tap **Phone app icon** .

2. Tap **menu icon** ⋮ located at the top of the screen.

3. Tap **Settings**.

4. Scroll down and tap **More settings**.

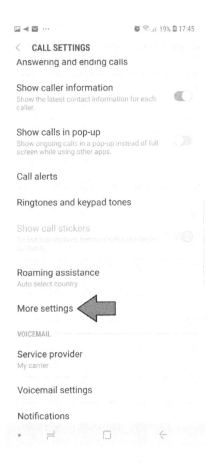

5. Tap **Show my caller ID** and choose an option.

Voicemail

Setting Up Voicemail

1. From the home screen, tap **Phone app icon** .

2. Tap the keyboard icon ⊞ if needed

3. Press and hold 1 and follow the prompts.

Please note that you might need to contact your network service provider to successfully set up a voicemail. For example, you might need to contact your network service provider to get a voicemail number or create a voicemail password.

Listening to Voicemail or Call Your Voicemail

1. To listen to your voicemail, open the Phone app.

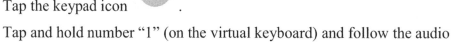

2. Tap the keypad icon   .

3. Tap and hold number "1" (on the virtual keyboard) and follow the audio instructions to listen to your voicemails.

If the instructions above do not work for you, please contact your network service provider to know how to listen to and manage your voicemails.

Managing Voicemail settings

1. From the home screen, tap **Phone app icon** .

2. Tap **menu icon** ⋮ located at the top of the screen.

3. Tap **Settings**.

4. If needed, scroll down and tap **Voicemail settings**.

5. Tap a setting to manage.

If your network provider supports it, you might be able to forward your unanswered calls to voicemail. To learn how to manage call forwarding options, please page 271. Please contact your network service provider to know how to forward calls to voicemail.

Using the Messaging app

This app allows you to send texts, images and video messages to other SMS and MMS devices.

To start or manage a conversation:

1. Tap the **Messages** app icon from the Home screen.

2. Tap the new message icon located at the bottom right corner of the screen.

3. Type in the first letters of the recipient's name. The list filters as you type. Then tap the required contact. Note; depending on your service provider, you can add up to 20 contacts (if not more). If you don't have the number on your contact, just key in the number in **Search Contacts or enter number** field (located at the top of the screen). To remove a contact from the send list, just tap the minus icon (-) next to the contact.

4. Tap the **Start** icon located at the top of the screen and write the text for your SMS/MMS.

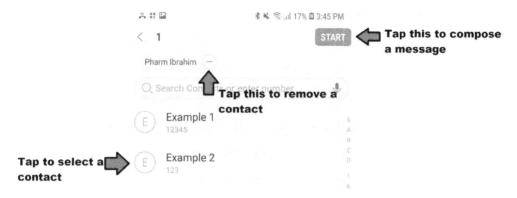

5. To attach a file such as audio, tap the plus icon and tap the menu icon (the three dots icon), Then choose an option.

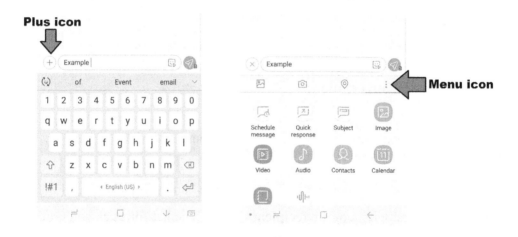

6. When you are done, tap the send icon　. If prompted, tap **Send**.

7. To reply a message, tap the message and enter a message in the reply field. Tap the send icon　when you are done.

8. To **Delete** a conversation, press and hold the message in question and tap on **Delete**. Select **Delete** when prompted.

9. In a conversation, you can press and hold a message to **forward, copy, share** or **delete** the message.

Delete

Copy text

Forward

Share

Star message

Send to Reminder

Copy to SIM 1

View details

Message options

- If you receive an attachment, you can tap on the attachment to view it. To save an attachment, tap and hold the attachment and select **Save attachment**. You can also tap the **Share** icon to share the attachment or **Delete** to delete an attachment. To view saved attachments, go to the app screen, tap **Samsung** folder, tap **My files** and tap a content category. Alternatively, visit **Photos/Gallery** app if the attachment is an image.

- To customize your message settings, from the message screen, tap the menu icon ⋮ and select **Settings.** Tap the desired setting to adjust. To access more settings, tap **More Settings.** *Please note that the features available on message settings may differ from one service provider to another.*

Notifications
Block numbers and messages
More settings
Privacy
About Messages

Message settings menu

- **You can block text messages** from certain numbers if your service provider supports this feature. To do this, Tap the menu icon ⋮ > **Settings** > **Block numbers and messages** > **Block numbers**. Then enter the desired number in the **Enter number** field and tap the + icon to add the number to the block list. To go into your contacts/ message inbox, tap **Contacts/Inbox**. To remove a number from the message block list, tap the minus (-) icon.

- When you receive a message, you can easily save the number if it is not yet saved in your contacts. To do this, tap the messaging app. Tap a conversation, tap the menu icon ⋮ located at the top right corner of the screen and tap the number in question. Thereafter, tap **Create contact** (located at the bottom of the screen). Follow the on-screen instructions to finish the process.

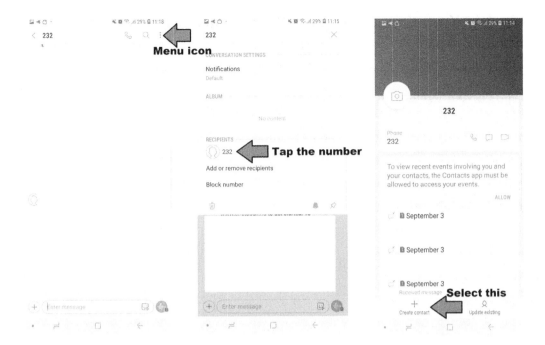

EMAIL APP

Introduction

Samsung Galaxy Note 9 comes preloaded with an email app for sending and receiving emails. One of the things you would need to do when you start using this device is to set up an email account. In this section of the guide, I would be discussing how to use your mail app like a maven.

How to Add Your Email Accounts to the Email app

You probably have many email accounts and you may wish to add these accounts to the email app on your device.

The email accounts you can add to the Email app include Google Mail and Yahoo Mail among others.

To add an email account:

1. Swipe down from the top of the screen and select settings icon ⚙ .

2. Tap **Cloud and accounts**.

3. Tap **Account.**

4. Tap **Add account.**

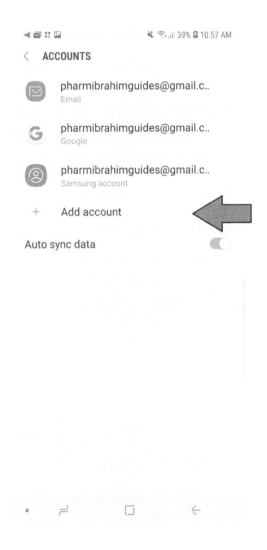

5. Tap **Email** and fill in the details.

6. To add another email account, repeats steps 1 to 5 above.

7. To add an Exchange account, select **Exchange** and follow the prompts. In addition, to add a Google account, tap **Google** and follow the prompts.

Special Note on Adding Exchange Account to the Email App

Following the instructions above might not be enough when you want to add your Exchange account to the Email app and you may need extra information. You may need to obtain from your Exchange administrator or provider the account's server address, domain name (and/or username) in addition to your email address and password.

How to Compose and Send an Email Message Using the Email App

You can easily send an email message to your friends or organization using the Email App. In this section of the guide, we would be exploring how to compose and send an email message.

To send an email message:

- From the Home screen, swipe up and tap **Email** . If you can't see the Email app, check **Samsung** folder on the application screen.
- If you are using the Email app for the first time, follow the prompts to get started.

- To change to another email account if multiple email accounts are configured, swipe right from the left edge of the screen and tap an account.

- To compose a new email, tap the new email icon located at the bottom of the screen.

- Tap the field next to **To** and type in the email address of the recipient. You can also tap the contact icon to view and add contacts.

- To send a copy to another person, tap the dropdown icon ⌄ next to **To** and type the person's email address in the **Cc/Bcc** field.

💡 Cc means Carbon Copy. If you use the Cc option to send a message to many recipients, all the recipients will see the message and all other email addresses that have received the message. On the other hand, Bcc stands for Blind Carbon Copy. If you use Bcc option to send a message to many recipients, all the recipients will see the message, but will not see other email addresses that have received the message.

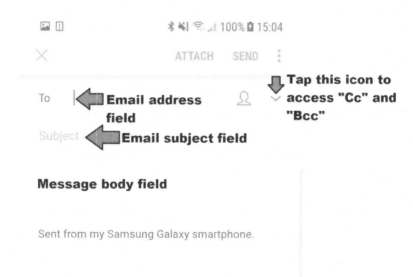

- If you have more than one email account configured on the Email app and you wish to send from a different email account, tap the dropdown icon next to **From** to choose a different email account. See the picture below.

- Tap **Subject** field and key in the subject of your email.
- Tap the text input field and write the text for your email.

- You can use the formatting tab at the bottom of the screen to perform the following actions:

1. **S Pen mode:** When you tap this icon, a writing pad would appear. Simply pick a writing color and begin to write your thoughts using the pad. When you are done, tap **Done** to save.

2. **Undo:** Tap to undo an action.

3. **Redo:** Tap to redo an action.

4. **Image:** Tap this to add an image.

5. **Font Size**: Use this option to change the font size of your text.

6. **Bold**: You can bolden a part or your entire message. To bolden a text, select the text(s) and tap the **B** icon.

7. **Italicize**: You can make your text appear italicized by clicking on the *I* icon.

8. **Underline**: Use the **U** icon to underline a text.

9. **Font color**: Tap this to change the font color.

10. **Font background color**: Tap this to change the font background color.

11. **Numbering**: Tap this to create a numbered list.

12. **Bullets**: Tap this to create a bullet list.

13. **Increase indent**: Tap this to move the paragraph farther away from the margin.

14. **Decrease indent**: Tap this to move the paragraph towards the margin.

To access more formatting options, swipe the formatting icons to the left or right. (See the arrows below).

- When you are satisfied with the message and you are ready to send it, tap **Send** located at the top of the Email app screen.

Before you can apply some of the formatting options above to a block of texts, you would need to select the texts. To do this, tap and hold a word and drag or to select the texts you want.

You could quickly save an email to Drafts folder by swiping down from center part of the screen. To access **Drafts** folder, open the Email app and swipe in from the left edge of the screen. Then tap **Drafts**.

Attaching a file

You can insert an attachment into your message by clicking on **ATTACH** located at the top of the screen. Select whether your attachment is a **DOCUMENT, a GALLERY,** or **OTHER (e.g. Samsung Notes).** Locate and tap on the file you want to attach.

Choose an option ➡ DOCUMENT   GALLERY   OTHER

To view saved attachments, go to app screen and tap **Samsung** folder. Tap **My files** and tap an appropriate content category. Alternatively, visit **Photos/Gallery** app if the attachment is an image.

Managing a Received Email

One of the most important functions of any email app is the ability to receive incoming messages. By default, Email app searches for new messages and alerts you when there is one.

New messages are either stored in Inbox or Spam folder and these are the two places to check if you are expecting an email. To access **Spam** folder, open the Email app and swipe in from the left edge of the screen. Then tap on **All Folders** and select **Spam**.

To see if there is a new message, swipe down from the top of the screen.

✗If you are not getting notifications from Email app, these are the things to check:

1. Check that you have not blocked notifications from this app. You can know this by following the steps on page 90.

2. Confirm that you have not disabled **Sync** function. To do this, swipe down from the top of the screen with two fingers. Then swipe left and see if **Sync** appears bold. If it appears bold, then it is enabled. Please note that if *Sync* is disabled you may not get some notifications.

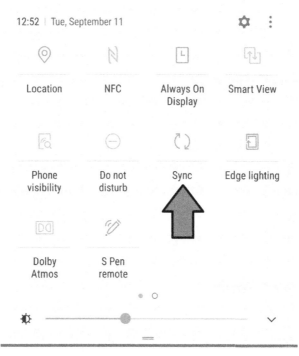

3. If the first two steps above do not work, then make sure your phone is not restricting the Email app's battery usage. Restricting the battery usage for an app might affect the ability of the app to get sync or use data. To know if Email app has a restricted battery usage, go to **Settings** ⚙ > **Apps** > **menu icon** (located at the top of the screen) > **Special access** > **Optimize battery usage**. Tap the dropdown menu and select **All apps** (see the picture below).

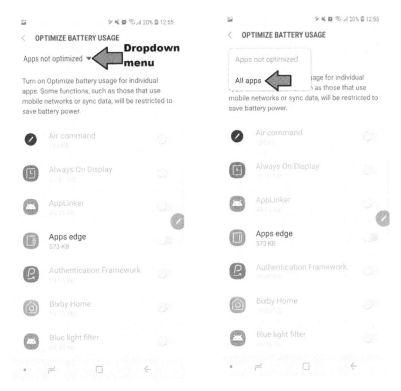

Scroll down and locate the **Email** app and make sure the indicator switch next to it is turned off.

To read a message:

- Tap on the subject of a message to open the message text in the preview pane.

- Those messages that you have not yet read should appear bold.

- A paperclip icon ⬿ means that a message has an attachment.

- The Email app allows you to perform the following actions on a message in your inbox:

If the icons above are not showing up while viewing an email message, swipe down from the middle of the screen.

1. **Reply:** Tap this button to reply an email message. When you tap this button, a new window appears. This window is similar to what appears when you tap on a new email button but with a slight difference. The reply window contains the recipient's name and the subject. In addition, the original message usually appears at the bottom of your reply for reference.

2. **Reply All:** If the message in your inbox is addressed to several people, you can choose to reply all those people by tapping **Reply All.** You can know whether an email is sent to many people by tapping **Details** tab next to the sender's name/address.

3. **Forward:** Use this option to send a copy of an email in your inbox to your friends or associates. When you tap on the **Forward** button, a message window with a subject line preceded by "Fwd:" appears. The original message address (To and From), date, subject, attachment, and text are also usually included. In addition, you will have the option to fill in the email address of the person to whom you are sending the message.

4. **Delete:** Use this option to delete a message from your inbox. Alternatively, tap and hold the email and select **Delete.**

5. **Thread:** This shows the number of conversations you have made. To see the list of conversations, tap this icon.

When you open the Email app inbox to check a mail, the name of the sender is usually displayed on the top of the message pane. To see the email address of whoever sent the message, tap the email and tap the name of the sender. Select **View contact**.

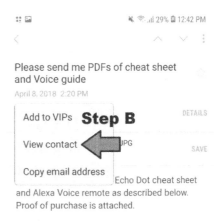

In addition, to quickly add an email address to VIP list, simply double tap the name of the sender or email address. To remove it from VIP list, double tap again.

How to Open and Save an Attachment in the Email App

The email with an attachment will have a paper clip icon displayed next to the address of the sender when you check your message inbox.

To open an attachment:

1. Tap the message that has the attachment as indicated by a paper clip icon .

2. When the message opens, tap **Save** next to the attachment to save it.

If your device does not have an appropriate program to open the attachment, you may be unable to view the attachment. In a situation like this, you would need to install the appropriate program for the file type. You may ask the person that sent the message about which program to use to open the attachment.

3. To view saved attachments, go to the app screen and tap **Samsung** folder. Tap **My files** and tap **Downloads**. Alternatively, if the attachment is an image, go to **Photos/Gallery** app.

Managing the Settings Options

- To access the Email app settings, open the Email app and tap menu icon located at the left top corner of the screen.

- Tap on **Settings** located at the top of the screen.

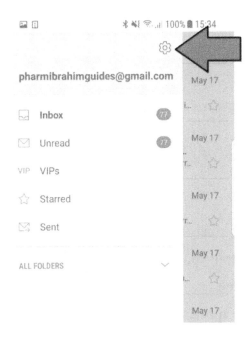

- Under **General** tab, tap an option.

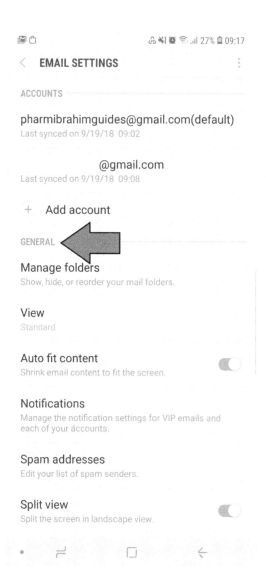

- To configure specific settings for an account, tap the account.

- To delete an account from your device, tap the email account and tap **REMOVE** next to the account name.

- To manage what name appears when you send a message using the Samsung Email app, tap **Your name** and enter appropriate name. Then tap **Done**.

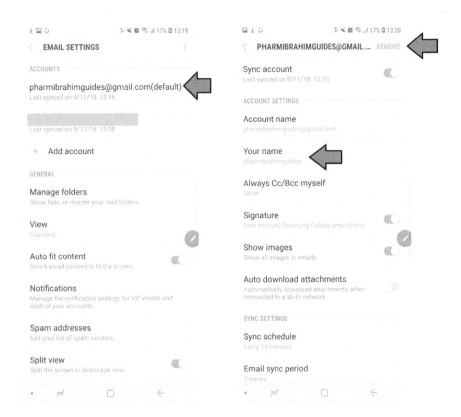

How to Remove the Default Email Signature in the Email App

You can use the Signature tab to command the Email app what signature to include in a

message. To do this, open the email app, tap the menu icon ⸻ (located at the top of the

screen) and tap **Settings** ⚙ . Tap the desired account, tap **Signature** and key in a

signature of your choice. Tap **DONE** located at the top of the screen. You can use the

switch next to Signature to enable or disable this feature.

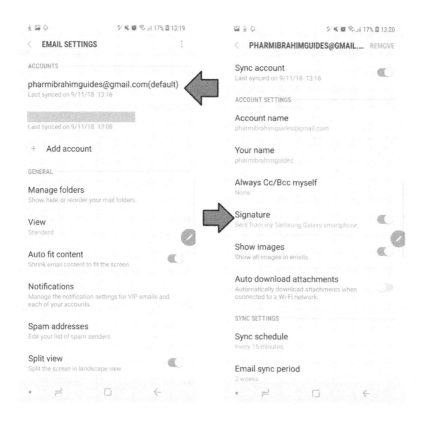

An email signature is a text that appears by default after the body of your message. You may set your email signature to be your name or brand.

Gmail App Demystified

Gmail gives you many features that makes it special. In this manual, you would learn how to use Gmail app like a pro. Let's get started!

How to Add Your Email Accounts to the Gmail App

You probably have many email accounts and you may wish to add these accounts to the Gmail app.

 If needed, you can download **Gmail** app from Google Play store.

To add an email account:

1. From the Home screen, tap on **Gmail** . If you are using the app for the first time, please follow the prompts.

2. To add your first email account, tap "Add email address", "Take me to Gmail" or "Add another email address" and enter your email account information.

3. To add another email account, tap the menu icon . Scroll down and tap **Settings**.

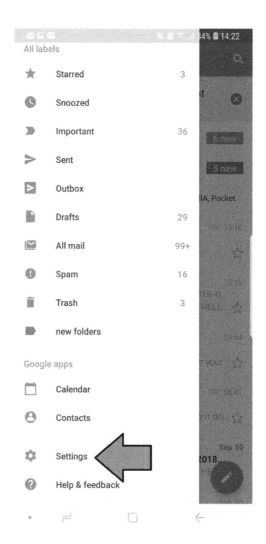

- Tap **Add account** and follow the prompts.

Special Note on Adding Exchange Account to Gmail App

Following the instructions above might not be enough when you want to add your Exchange account to Gmail app and you may need extra information. You may need to obtain from your Exchange administrator or provider the account's server address, domain/user name, in addition to your email address and password.

How to Compose and Send an Email Message Using Gmail App

You can easily send an email message to your friends or organization using the Gmail app. In this section of the guide, we would be exploring how to compose and send an email message.

To compose and send an email message:

- From the Home screen, swipe up and tap **Gmail** .

- To change to another email account if multiple email accounts are configured, tap the menu icon and tap the account presently selected. Then tap the account you want to view.

Tap the account presently selected and then tap an account from the option that appears

- To compose a new email, tap the new email icon located at the bottom of the screen.

- Tap the field next to the "**To**" field and type in the email address of the recipient. If enabled, as you type an email address, Gmail will suggest email addresses based on your contacts. To add another email address, simply type the email address into the "To" field. You may separate each email address with a coma. To delete/remove an email address from the "To" field, tap the email address and tap the **X** icon.

- To send a copy to another person, tap the dropdown icon ˅ next to the "**To**" field and type the person's email address in the **Cc/Bcc** field.

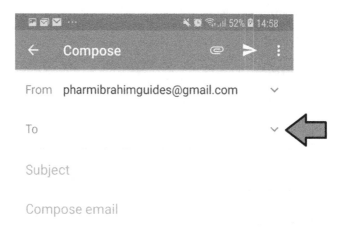

To know what Cc and Bcc stands for, please refer to the tip on page 285.

- If you have more than one email account configured on Gmail app and you wish to send from a different email account, tap the dropdown icon next to "**From**" to choose a different email account. See the picture above.
- Tap **Subject** field and key in the subject of your email.

- Tap the text input field and type the texts for your email.

- To format a block of texts, select the texts by tapping and holding a word and drag 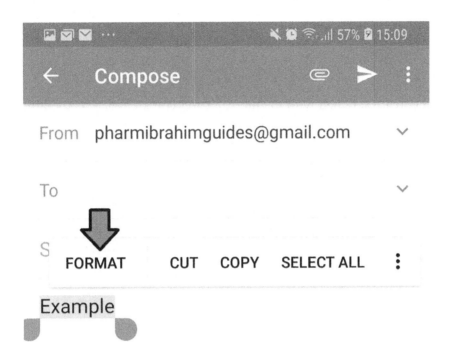 or to select the texts you want. Then select **Format** from the options that appear.

You can use the formatting tab at the bottom of the screen to perform the following actions:

1. **Bold**: You can bolden a part or your entire message using this feature. To bolden a text, select the text(s) and tap the **B** icon.

2. **Italicize**: You can make your text appear italicized by clicking on the *I* icon.

3. **Underline**: Use the <u>U</u> icon to underline a text.

4. **Font color**: Tap this to change the font color.

5. **Font background color**: Tap this to change the font background color.

6. **Remove Formatting:** Tap this to remove any format you have given to a text or block of texts.

7. **Close:** Tap this to close the formatting dialogue box.

- When you are satisfied with the message and you are ready to send it, tap **Send** located at the top of the Gmail app screen.

- To save a message as draft, tap the menu icon located at the top of the screen and select **Save Draft**. Please note that you may need to fill the "**To**" field or the body of the message before you can save a message as draft. On the other hand, to discard a message, tap the menu icon and select **Discard**.

Before you can apply some of the formatting options above to a block of texts, you would need to select the texts. To do this, tap and hold a word, then drag or to select the texts you want.

Attaching a File

You can insert an attachment into your message by clicking on the attachment icon located at the top of the screen. This opens a dialog box. Choose from **Attach file** or **Insert from Drive**. Then locate and tap on the file you want to attach.

Managing a Received Email

One of the most important functions of any email app is the ability to receive incoming messages. By default, Gmail app searches for new messages and alerts you when there is a message(s).

New messages are either stored in Inbox or Spam folder and these are the places to check if you are expecting an email. To access Spam folder, tap the menu icon , scroll down and tap **Spam** folder. Alternatively, swipe from the left edge of the screen towards the middle to access Spam folder.

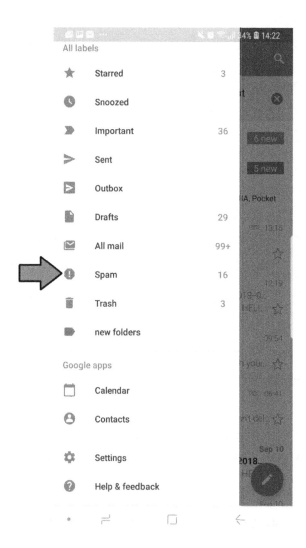

To see if there is a new message, swipe down from the top of the Gmail app's screen.

To read/manage a message:

Please note that some options discussed below might not be available on your phone. The options you see are dependent on the type of email account you are using. I have noticed that you will see a more robust set of options when you are using a Gmail account with Gmail app.

- Tap the subject of the message to open the message text in the preview pane.

- Unread messages should appear bold.

- The attachment icon means that a message has an attachment.

- To make a message your favorite, tap the star icon ☆ located at the top right corner of the screen.

- To reply a message, scroll down on the message (if necessary) and tap **Reply**. If the email was sent to more than one person, you can tap **Reply all** to send the reply to all those who have received the message. To forward the message, tap

  Forward. While composing a reply message, you can tap the menu icon ⋮ (located at the top of the screen) to discard a message, save a message as draft or add an email address from the Contact app.

find more info here and in our
updated terms and conditions.

Your Office 365 Home subscription
will automatically update in 30 days,
so you don't need to do anything.
You're agreeing to this update by
continuing your subscription.

Thanks for being an Office 365
customer.

This email was sent from an unmonitored mailbox.

You are receiving this email because you have subscribed to
Microsoft Office 365.
Privacy Statement

Microsoft Corporation, One Microsoft Way, Redmond, WA
98052 USA

Microsoft

Reply   Reply all   Forward

- To quickly delete a message, tap the delete icon located at the top of the screen.

- To move a message to another folder, tap the menu icon and select **Move to**. Then select the folder.

- To archive a message, tap the archive icon located at the top of the screen. To access archived messages, tap the menu icon (located at the top left corner of the screen) and tap **All mail**. Please note that when you archive a message, the message will come back to your inbox when someone replies.

- To access the details of a sender of an email, tap **View details** next to the sender's name. This allows you to see details like email address.

- To go back to inbox, while viewing a message, tap the inbox icon.

You might like to customize what happens when you swipe the screen while viewing the message list in your inbox. To do this, please refer to the tip on page 320.

Using the Gmail In-App Inbox Menu icons

When you tap a message in your inbox, you will usually see two menu icons. These icons allow you to customize your messages. To access these menu icons,

- Open the Gmail app and tap a message from your inbox.
- Tap a menu icon (see the picture below).

Tap the first menu icon to access the following:

Please note that the options you see when you tap the menu icon is dependent on the type of email account you are using. I have noticed that you will see a more robust options when you are using a Gmail account.

1. **Move to:** Choose this option to move an email to another folder.

2. **Snooze:** When you tap "Snooze", you will be able to hide the message concerned in snoozed folder for a period of time. When you snooze a message, it is removed from the inbox and put inside the "snoozed" folder for a chosen time. To access Snoozed folder, if needed, tap the back arrow icon ← (located at the top of the screen) and tap the menu icon ≡ (located at the top left corner of the screen). Tap **Snoozed**.

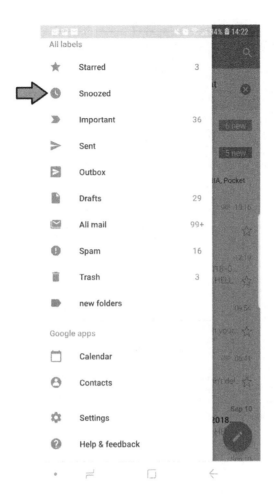

To unsnooze, open the snoozed folder, tap the message you want to unsnooze and tap

the menu icon ⋮ . Then tap **Unsnooze.** *A snoozed email message would appear at the top of your emails after the snooze time elapses.*

Please note that you may not be able to use Snooze option if you are not using a Gmail account.

3. **Change labels:** When you change the label of an email, you move/copy the email to a new location. To change a label, select **Change labels** and tick a folder you like (you can uncheck the label you don't want). Then tap **OK.**

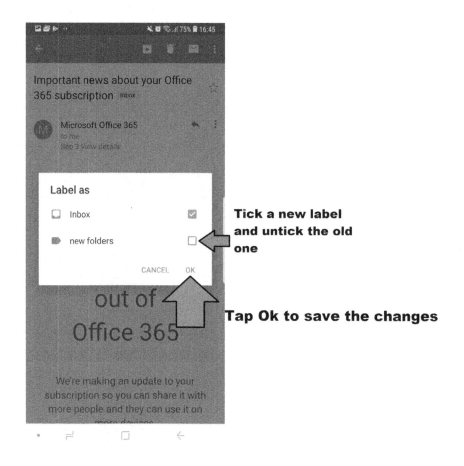

Tick a new label and untick the old one

Tap Ok to save the changes

4. **Mark Important:** Any message you find very dear to you, mark it as important. To mark a message as important, tap **Mark Important**. To access "Important" folder, tap the back arrow 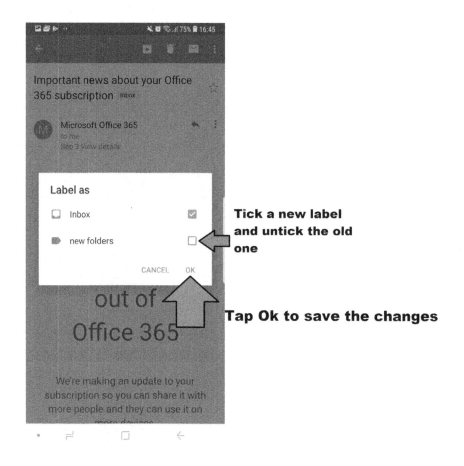 (if needed) and tap the menu icon . Then tap **Important**.

5. **Unsubscribe**: Gmail app allows you to unsubscribe from some emails using this option. To unsubscribe from an email list, simply tap **Unsubscribe**. Tap **Unsubscribe** again to confirm.

6. **Mute:** You can mute a message to prevent it from appearing in your main inbox. To access your muted messages, tap the menu icon . Tap **All mail**. Please note

that when you mute a message, the message may not come back to your inbox when someone replies.

7. **Print:** Use this option to print an email or save an email as a PDF. To use this option to save an email as PDF, tap **Print.** Tap the dropdown arrow and select **Save as PDF** (if needed). Thereafter, tap the yellow **PDF** icon and choose a folder. Then tap **Done** to download.

8. **Revert auto-sizing:** If you are viewing an email in your inbox and it is not appearing as it should, you can tap on **Revert auto-sizing** to see if this solves the problem. *Note that this option is not always available.*

9. **Report Spam:** If you believe that an email message is a spam, you can report it to Google using this option.

Tap the second menu icon ⋮ to access the following:

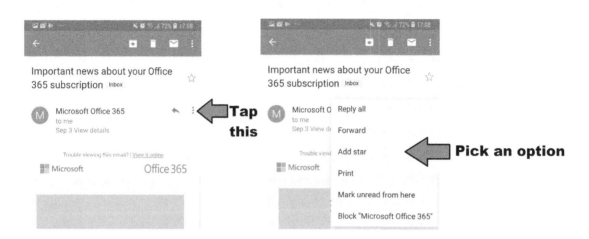

Please note that the options you see when you tap the (second) menu icon is dependent on the type of email account you are using. I have noticed that you will see a more robust set of options when you are using a Gmail account.

- **Reply all**: If an email is sent to more than one person, you can tap **Reply all** to reply to all those who have received the message.
- **Add star (Make an email message your favorite)**: If you want to make a message your favorite, tap **Add star**. To view your starred message, tap the back arrow (located at the top of the screen) and tap the menu icon ☰ (located at the top left corner of the screen). Tap **Starred**.
- **Print:** Please refer to page 313 to learn how to manage print options.
- **Mark unread from here**: If you want a message to appear bold (as if it is unread), tap "Mark unread from here".
- **Block** …: If you don't want future messages from a contact to be delivered to your inbox, tap **Block...**

Please note that any future message from a blocked contact will be marked as spam. To unblock a contact, tap the menu icon ⋮ again and select **Unblock...**

How to Open and Save an Attachment in Email App

The email with an attachment should have a paper clip icon 📎 displayed next to the address of the sender when you check your message inbox.

To open/manage an attachment:

1. Tap the message that has the attachment, as indicated by a paper clip 📎.
2. When the message opens, tap the attachment that you want to open. To save the attachment, tap the menu icon ⋮ and select **Save**. If your device does not have an appropriate program to open the attachment, you may be unable to view the attachment. In a situation like this, you would need to install the appropriate app for the file type. You may ask the person that sent the message about the app to use to open the attachment.
3. To view saved/downloaded attachments, go to applications screen and tap **Samsung** folder. Then tap **My Files** and select **Download**. Alternatively, you can double-tap the status bar (the bar at the top of the screen where icons such as Wi-Fi icon usually appear) to view your recent downloads. Then tap the downloaded file you want to view.

💡 If you want a smart file management app on your phone, you may consider installing **Files Go by Google** from Google Play store.

In addition, you can prevent Gmail from automatically downloading an attachment when connected to Wi-Fi. To do this:

1. Open the Gmail app.

2. Tap the menu icon 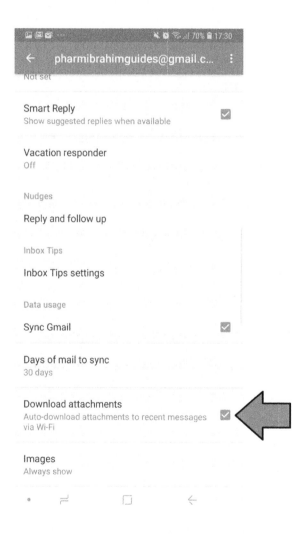 (located at the top left corner of the screen).

3. Scroll down the email options and tap **Settings.**

4. Tap an email account.

5. Scroll down and uncheck the box next to **Download attachments.**

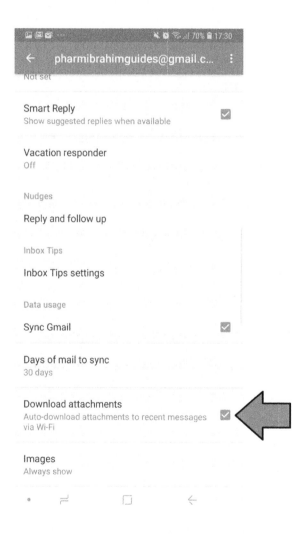

Unsubscribing from an Email List

If you will like to unsubscribe from any email list, please follow the steps highlighted below:

- Open the message you want to unsubscribe from.

- Tap the menu icon ⋮ .

- Select **Unsubscribe.**
- Tap **Unsubscribe** again to confirm.

Blocking an email address

If an email address is disturbing you with unwanted emails, you can block the email address. To do this:

- Open the message in question.

- Tap the menu icon ⋮ .

- Select **Block...**

Please note that any future message from a blocked contact will be marked as spam. To unblock a contact, tap the menu icon ⋮ again and select **Unblock...**

Cleaning Up Your Inbox

Overtime, inbox usually grows to contain thousands of irrelevant messages. If this is your situation and you wish to clean your inbox so that it contains only the most important messages, please follow the instructions below:

1. Open the Gmail app and look for those emails that contain the most irrelevant/unwanted messages. Open one of these emails and block the sender's address. Repeat this step for all the annoying email messages. Please see page 317 to know how to block a sender.

2. Then go back to your inbox and select all the irrelevant/unwanted messages. To select a message, tap and hold the message for one second and lift your finger. Repeat this method to select all the irrelevant/unwanted messages. If you mistakenly select a message, tap and hold the message for one second and lift your finger to unselect it. Then tap the delete icon 🗑 (located at the top of the screen)

to send the selected messages to Trash folder. *Please note that items that have been in Trash folder for more than 30 days will be deleted (automatically).*

Tap the Delete icon to move the selected messages to Trash folder

Tap, hold and lift your finger to select a message

3. Go back to your inbox and select all the very important messages following the method mentioned in step 2. Then tap the menu icon ⋮ (located at the top of the screen) and select **Mark important**. To access "Important" folder, tap the menu icon ▤ and tap **Important**. Please note that if you mark a message as important, the message remains in your primary inbox.

4. Go back to your inbox and select all social/promotional messages following the method mentioned in step 2. Then tap the menu icon ⋮ (located at the top of the screen) and select **Move to**. Select Social or Promotions. To access Social or Promotions folder, tap the menu icon ▤ and tap **Social/Promotions**.

5. Finally, go back to your inbox and tap the menu icon ▤. Tap **Settings** and tap an account. Then tap **Inbox categories**. Make sure the checkbox next to **Update** is selected. When this is selected, Gmail will automatically put auto-generated updates including receipts, bills and statements in (Updates) folder. This should allow you to find your bills and statements faster in the future. You may also check

the box next to **Forums** if you want messages from online groups, discussion boards and mailing lists to be put in one folder.

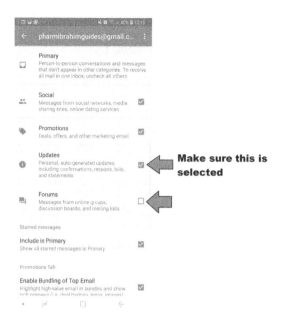

*After doing all the five steps highlighted above, you would see that your **Primary** folder would contain fewer messages (because some of the messages would have been moved to **Updates/Forum** folder).*

Please note that, if you have several thousands of emails, it may take time before you can clean up your inbox. If this is your situation, I would advise you clean up your inbox little by little so as not to be overwhelmed. In addition, if you can, make sure you decide the fate of your future messages within 72 hours of receiving. Try to delete an unwanted message as soon as you read it. Don't wait for it to become a concern before you send a useless message to the trash bin.

💡 You might like to customize what happens when you swipe the screen while viewing conversation list in your inbox, to do this:

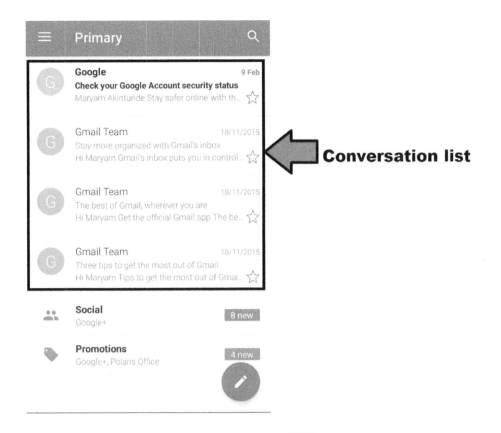

Conversation list

1. Open the Gmail app and tap the menu icon ☰. Tap on **Settings**.

2. Tap **General settings**.

3. Tap **Swipe actions**.

4. Tap **Change** next to **Right swipe** and pick an option.

5. Tap **Change** next to **Left swipe** and pick an option.

Searching the Gmail App

To avoid wasting time, you can use the search option in the Gmail app to quickly find emails. When looking for an email, using the search tab is usually the best option if you know the right search phrase to use.

To use the search feature:

1. Open the Gmail app.

2. Tap the search icon (located at the top of the screen).

3. Enter a search phrase and tap the lens icon or the **Done** button on the on-screen keyboard.

To delete your Gmail search history:

1. Open the Gmail app.

2. Tap the menu icon .

3. Scroll down the email options and tap **Settings.**

4. Tap **General settings.**

5. Tap the menu icon (located at the top of the screen).

6. Tap **Clear search history**.

Stop Picture from Being Automatically Displayed

If you have allowed images to be displayed from a sender while viewing an email message, you can follow the steps mentioned below to revoke this approval.

1. Repeat steps 1 to 5 under "To delete your Gmail search history" above.

2. Tap **Clear picture approvals**.

💡 You can prevent images from being shown inside your email messages. To do this, repeat steps 1 to 3 under "To delete your Gmail search history" above. Tap an email account, then scroll down and tap **Images**. Select **Ask before showing**.

Using Vacation Responder

If you are on a vacation, you can enable Gmail to auto-respond to people that message you during this time.

Please note that the Vacation Responder might not be available if you are not using a Gmail account.

In addition, normally, messages categorized as spam and messages addressed to mailing list (you subscribe to) won't get response from the vacation responder.

To use vacation responder:

1. Open the Gmail app.

2. Tap the menu icon 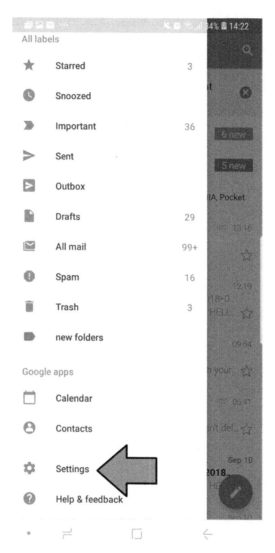 (located at the top left corner of the screen).

3. Scroll down the email options and tap **Settings**.

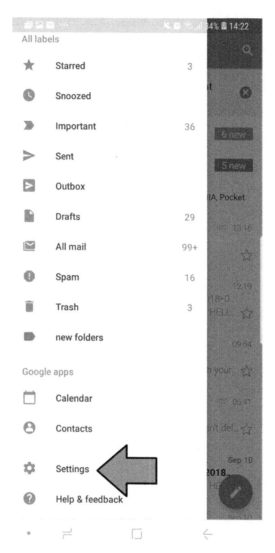

4. Tap an email account.

5. Tap **Vacation responder**.

6. Tap the status switch next to **Vacation responder** and fill in necessary information.

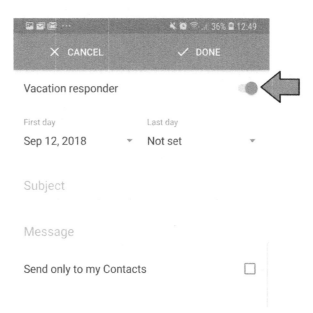

7. If you want Gmail to message only your contacts, tap the checkbox next to **Send only to my Contacts**.

8. Tap **Done** located at the top of the screen to save the changes.

Managing the Settings Options

Some of the options under Email Settings have already been discussed. But I would like to briefly mention few more things.

1. To access the Email app settings, open the Gmail app and tap the menu icon ☰ (located at the top left corner of the screen). Tap on **Settings**.

2. Tap an email account and tap an option of your choice. For example, to disable email notification, tap **Notifications** and the select **None**.

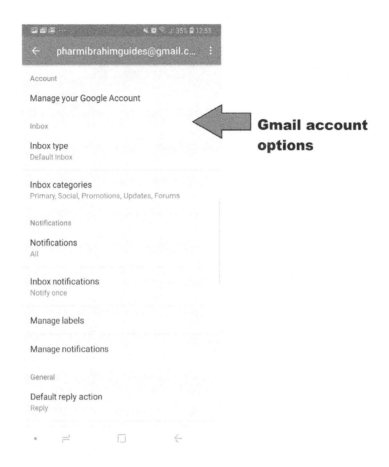

Gmail account options

💡 You might notice that if you tap on weblinks while reading an email, it opens in Gmail app. If you want to disable this feature so that the weblink can be opened using a web browser, perform the following actions:

a. Open the Gmail app and tap the menu icon ☰. Tap on **Settings**.

b. Tap **General settings**.

c. Uncheck the box next to **Open web links in Gmail**.

Deleting an Email Account

To delete an email account:

1. Swipe down from the top of the screen and select settings icon ⚙ .

2. Tap **Cloud and accounts**.

3. Tap **Account**.

4. Select the (Google) account you want to remove.

5. Tap **Remove Account**. Select **Remove Account** to confirm your choice.

Managing Email Signature

You can use the Signature tab to tell Gmail app what signature to include in a message. You can also edit signature message under this tab. To go to Signature settings, open the Gmail app and tap the menu icon ☰. Tap on **Settings**. Tap the desired account and tap **Mobile signature**. Type in the signature you want and tap **OK.**

An email signature is a text that appears by default after the body of your message. You may set your email signature to be your name or your brand.

Personal Information

Contacts

This app allows you to create and manage a list of your personal or business contacts. You can save names, mobile phone numbers, home phone numbers, email addresses and more.

Creating a contact

1. While on the Home screen, swipe up and tap on **Contact** app. If you are using the Contacts app for the first time, follow the onscreen instructions to set it up.

2. Tap on **Add contact** icon located at the lower right corner of the screen.

3. Select where you want to save the contact from the options that appear. To make your selection the default selection, tap **Set As Default.**

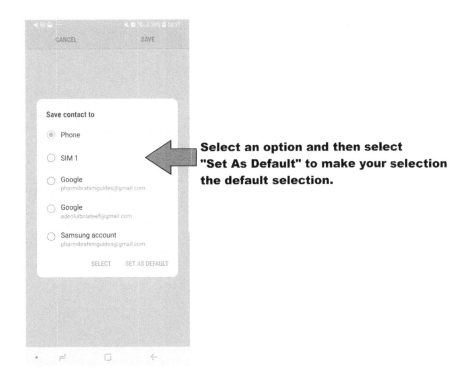

Select an option and then select "Set As Default" to make your selection the default selection.

To change your selection afterward, tap the dropdown arrow next to your selection. See the picture below.

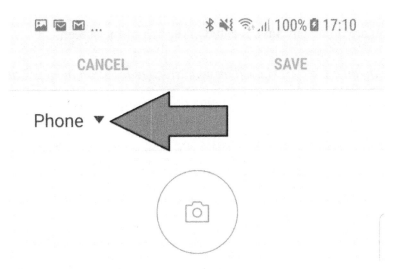

4. Fill in the details by tapping on each item on the screen.
5. To assign a contact to a group, tap **Group.**
6. To access more options, tap on **View more**.

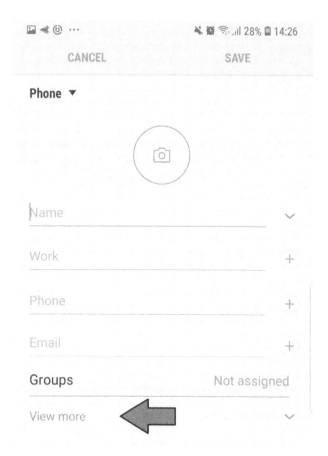

7. When you are done, tap **Save** located at the top of the screen.

Please note that if you choose SIM card as your storage location in step 3 above, you may not be able to fill more than a name and phone number.

To search for a contact, open the contact app and tap the **search** bar (located at the top of the screen). Start typing a name. The list filters as you type.

When you receive a message, you can easily save the number if it is not yet saved on your contacts list. To do this, tap the messaging app. Tap a conversation, tap the menu icon located at the top right corner of the screen and tap the phone number in question. Thereafter, tap **Create contact** (located at the bottom of the screen). Follow the on-screen instructions to finish the process.

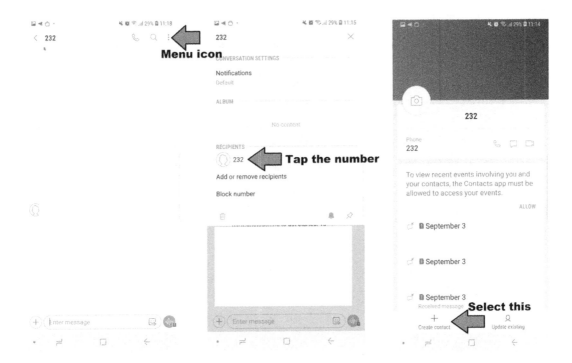

Menu icon

Tap the number

Select this

Managing Contacts

1. From the app screen, tap on the **Contact** app.

2. Tap on a contact from the list.

3. Tap the **details** icon (the last icon on the right).

4. To edit a contact, tap **EDIT** located at the top of the screen and enter the new details. Tap **Save** when you are done.

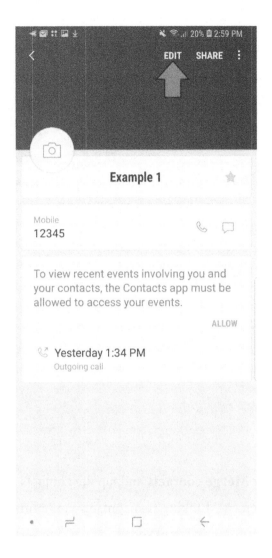

Please note that you might not be able to change the storage location of a contact using the editing option. If you need to change the storage location of a contact, I would advise you consider copying the contact to the new location. To know how to copy a contact, please see page 335.

5. To delete a contact, open the contact app, tap and hold the contact you want to delete, then tap on **Delete** located at the top of the screen. You can also use this method to delete many contacts at once. All you have to do is to select all the contacts you want to delete, then tap **Delete**.

6. To share a contact, tap and hold the contact you want to share, then tap **Share.**

To link a contact, tap the contact, tap **Details** and tap the menu icon ⋮ .

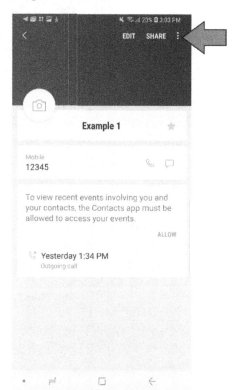

Then tap **Link contacts** or **Merge contacts** and tap the contacts to link with. Tap **Link** (located at the top of the screen). Linking two contacts is important if you have separate entries for the same contact from different social networking services or email accounts. To unlink a contact, tap the contact you want to unlink, tap **Details** and tap the menu icon

⋮ . Tap **Managed Link contacts** and tap the **Unlink** next to the contact you want to unlink. To link another contact, tap **Link Another Contact**. If you have many contacts linked together, tap **Unlink All** (located at the bottom of the screen) to unlink all of them.

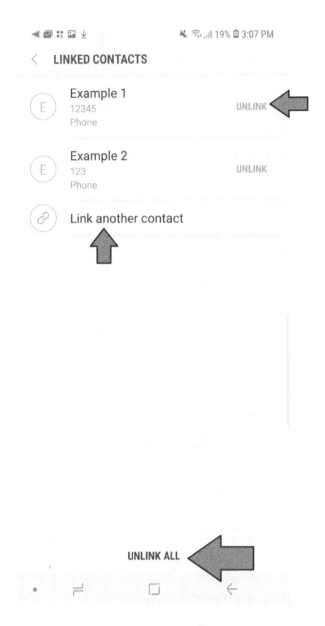

Please note that unlinking a contact does not delete the contact.

Copy contact(s)

If you have some contacts stored on your SIM card, you can copy them to your phone with some simple steps.

1. From the app screen, tap on the **Contact** app.

2. Tap the menu icon ⋮ .

3. Tap **Manage contacts**.

4. Tap **Import/Export contacts**.

5. Tap **Import**.

6. Select where you want to copy the contact(s) from.

7. If you want to import all the contacts, tap **ALL** located at the top of the screen. You may also individually select the contacts. To remove a contact you have previously selected, tap the minus icon next to it.

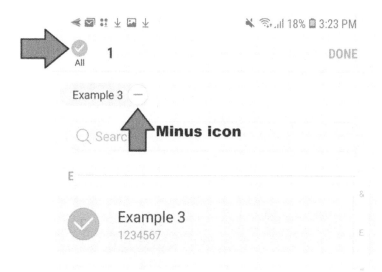

8. Tap **DONE** (located at the top of the screen).

9. Tap **Phone** or where you are sending the contacts to.

10. Tap **Import.** Please note that you can use this method to also copy contacts from SD card and internal storage.

You can **export** contacts from your phone to other places by following the steps similar to the ones mentioned above. But don't forget that you will select **Export** (and not Import) in step 5.

Contact Group

If you would like to send a message to several people at the same time, I would advise that you create a contact group. You can create a contact group for friends and family members in order to reach them easily.

To create a group:

1. From the app screen, tap on the **Contact** app.

2. Tap on **Groups.**

3. Tap **Create**.

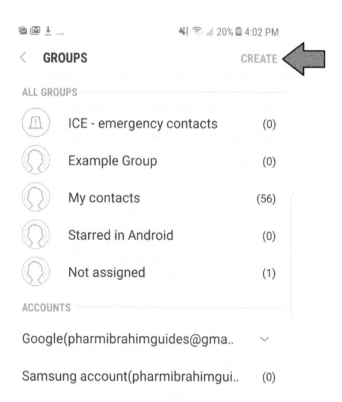

4. Fill in a name for the group, tap **Add member** to add members to the newly created group and tap **Done**.

5. To remove a contact, tap the minus icon next to the contact.

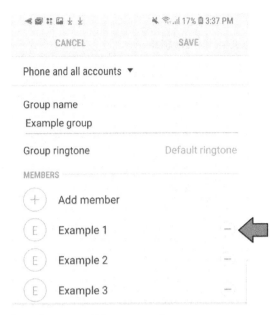

6. Tap **Save** (located at the top of the screen).

Please note that you may not be able to add contacts stored on SIM card to a contact group.

To add members to a group afterwards:

1. From the app screen, tap on **Contact** app.
2. Tap on **Groups** and tap a group.
3. Tap **Edit.**

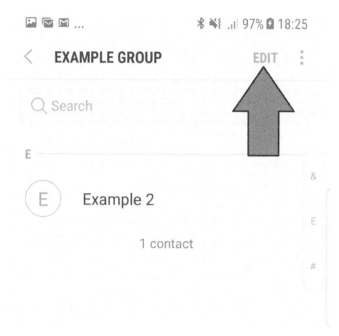

4. Tap **Add Member**. Then tap on a contact to add and tap **Done**.

5. Tap **Save** (located at the top of the screen) to save the changes.

To remove a contact from a group, follow steps 1 to 3 above, then tap the minus icon

next to the contact you want to remove.

Managing a group contact:

1. From the app screen, tap on the **Contact** app.

2. Tap on **Groups** and tap a group.

3. To send a message to a group, tap **Menu icon** ⋮ and tap **Send message**.

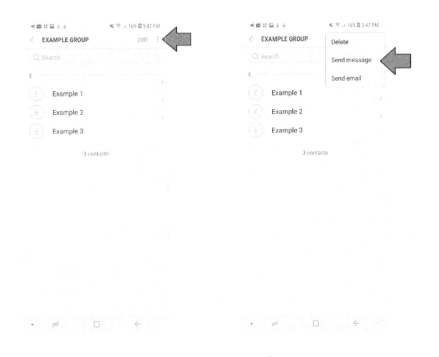

4. To send an email to a group, tap **Menu icon** ⋮ and tap **Send email**. Please note that you may not be able to send email to a group if you have not added email addresses to the individual contacts in the group.

Deleting a group:

1. From the app screen, tap on the **Contact** app.
2. Tap on **Groups** and tap a group.
3. Tap **Menu icon** ⋮ .
4. Tap **Delete**.
5. Tap **Group only** to delete only the group. Tap **Group and members** to delete both the group and the contact(s) in the group.

To customize the Contact app, tap on the **Contact** app, tap the **Menu icon** and tap **Settings**.

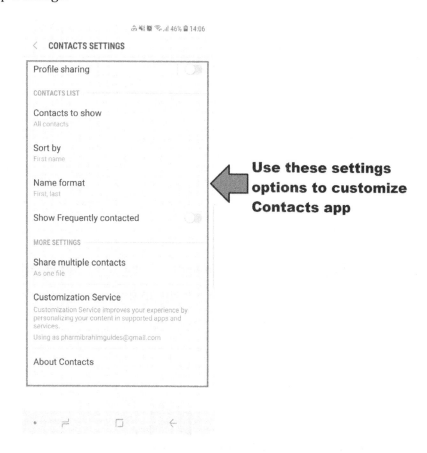

Use these settings options to customize Contacts app

In addition, you can change the default storage for your contacts if need be. To do this:

1. From the app screen, tap on the **Contact** app.

2. Tap the menu icon located at the top of the screen.

3. Tap **Manage contacts**.

4. Tap **Default storage location** and choose a new location.

Accessibility Features– the Special Features for Easy Usage

Accessibility services are special features for those with physical challenges. In addition, it provides you the opportunity to control your phone in a special way.

Vision

This option allows you to hear what is happening on the screen as you touch/interact with the phone screen.

To use the vision settings:

1. Swipe down from the top of the screen and select the settings icon .
2. Scroll down and tap **Accessibility**.
3. Tap **Vision**.
4. Tap the desired option. Interestingly, for complex options, usually, there are explanations beneath them. You can read these explanations to get what each option represents.

Vision tab contains those settings that help with vision. These settings are particularly good for visually impaired person.

Hearing

This tab allows you to control sound related settings. For example, you can turn off all sounds using this feature.

To use the Hearing settings:

1. Swipe down from the top of the screen and select the settings icon .

2. Scroll down and tap **Accessibility.**

3. Tap **Hearing.**

4. Tap the desired option. Interestingly, for complex options, usually, there are explanations beneath them. You can read these explanations to get what each option represents.

The settings under the hearing tab is particularly good for hearing impaired person. For example, you can turn on the flash notification if you want your phone to flash its light when there is a notification.

In addition, you can customize your phone to alert you when your baby is crying or when the doorbell is making a sound. This is a cool feature *but should be used responsibly*. To use this feature, repeat steps 1 to 3 under "To use the Hearing settings". Then tap **Sound detectors** and select an option. Carefully read the message that appears and tap **Confirm** if you agree.

Dexterity and Interaction

This option allows you to control your device in a special way. For example, you can control your device with your customized switches using the **Universal switches** tab. Although, I would advise you don't tamper with the **Universal switches** unless you know much about it. If you mistakenly switch on **Universal switches** and you wish to turn it off, just press the power button and the volume up button simultaneously once.

To use Dexterity and interaction:

1. Swipe down from the top of the screen and select the settings icon .
2. Scroll down and tap **Accessibility**.
3. Tap **Dexterity and interaction**.
4. Tap the desired option. Interestingly, for complex options, usually, there are explanations beneath them. You can read these explanations to get what each option represents.

Dexterity and interaction tab contains those settings that help you to control your device with gestures.

In addition, you can control how long your tap and hold the screen before you get a response. To do this, while in **Dexterity and Interaction**, tap **Touch and hold delay** and choose an option.

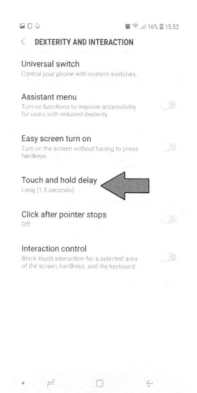

More settings

This option allows you to access extra accessibility settings. For example, you can export your accessibility settings and share them with another device using the settings (**Accessibility settings backup**) under this tab.

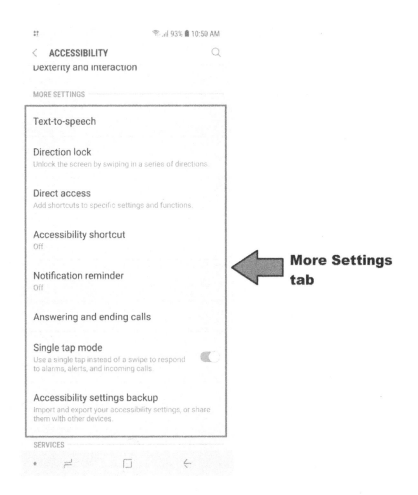

More Settings tab

You can end a call by pressing the power button. To do this, tap **Answering and ending calls** (see the picture above) and tap the status switch next to **Press Power key to end calls**.

Also, you can get reminded at a chosen interval if you have unread notifications. To do this, tap **Notification reminder** (see the picture above) and tap the status switch next to **ON**. If prompted, tap **Turn On** to confirm. Then tap **Reminder interval** and choose an option. To control which app you receive notification from, tap the status switch next to the app.

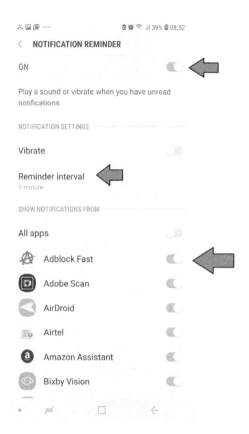

Services

This tab allows you to access/manage additional accessibility app(s). Any accessibility app downloaded from Google Play store should appear here.

TOOLS

Easy Mode

Easy mode provides a simpler layout and bigger icons on the Home screen, thereby enhancing visual experience and easier use. Please note that some features may not be available when Easy mode is enabled.

To enable and manage Easy mode:

1. Swipe down from the top of the screen and select the settings icon . Tap **Display** tab.
2. Tap **Easy mode**.
3. Tap **Easy mode** to enable this feature.
4. Tap **Done** located at the top of the screen to save your settings. Then tap the Home button to return to the Home screen.
5. When Easy mode is enabled, you can add a shortcut to your favorite contacts. To add a shortcut to a contact, from the Home screen, swipe the screen to the right. Then tap the plus icon and follow the prompts.

Tap this icon to add a
contact to the home
screen

To disable Easy mode:

1. Swipe down from the top of the screen and select the settings icon ⚙ . Tap
   Display tab.
2. Scroll down and tap **Easy mode**.
3. Tap **Standard mode** to exit Easy mode.
4. Tap **Done** to effect the changes.

Do Not Disturb

Do not disturb gives you the opportunity to prevent unnecessary disturbances from your phone. To quickly access this feature and customize it, swipe down from the top of the screen using two fingers, then tap and hold **Do Not disturb** for two seconds. Please note that you may need to swipe to the right to access more quick settings options before you can see **Do Not disturb** icon.

Then select an option.

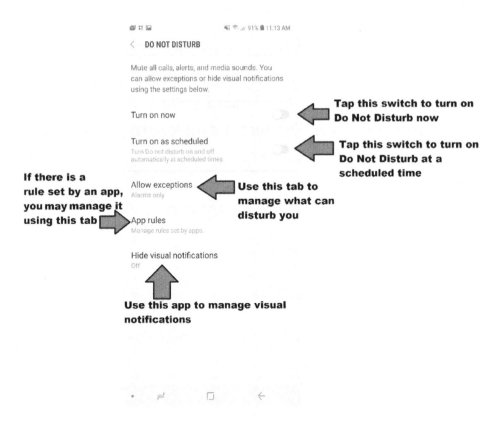

Tap this switch to turn on Do Not Disturb now

Tap this switch to turn on Do Not Disturb at a scheduled time

If there is a rule set by an app, you may manage it using this tab

Use this tab to manage what can disturb you

Use this app to manage visual notifications

If you choose to schedule Do Not Disturb, then use **Days** and **Set schedule** to customize your experience. Thereafter, tap the back button to save the changes.

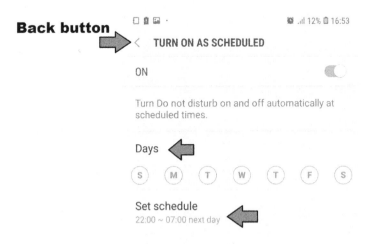

Back button

There is a feature on your phone called **Blue Light Filter**. Samsung claims this feature can help you sleep better. If you are having difficulty sleeping while using your phone, you may try using this feature. To use this feature:

Swipe down from the top of the screen and tap the settings icon > **Display** > **Blue Light Filter** > **Turn on now**.

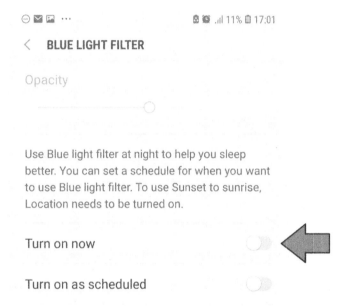

To schedule Blue Light Filter, tap the switch next to **Turn on as scheduled** and the choose an option.

Creating Schedules and More with the Calendar App

Your phone provides you with **Calendar** app to help you organize your schedules and tasks more conveniently and effectively. You can create schedules and add events.

Creating an event

1. From the Home screen, swipe up and tap on **Calendar** .

2. Tap the plus icon at the lower right side of the screen and enter the details.

3. To set the start and the end date of the event, tap **Start/End.**

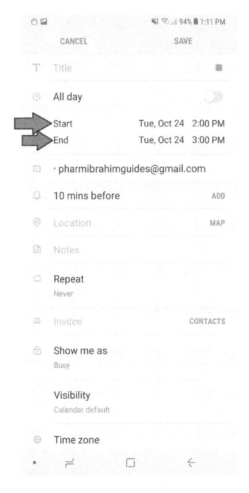

4. When you are done, tap **Save** (located at the top of the screen).

💡 Your phone will give you a notification when the time for an event comes.

Changing your calendar view

1. From the Home screen, swipe up and tap on **Calendar** .

2. To change the calendar view, tap **View** (located at the top of the screen). Tap the desired view.

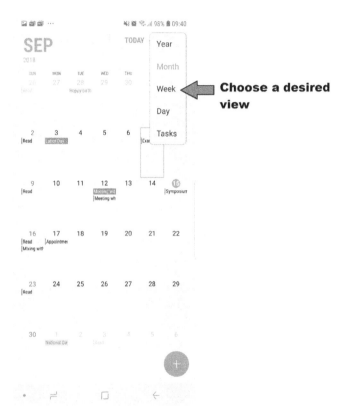

Viewing an event/schedule

1. From the Home screen, swipe up and tap on **Calendar** .

2. To change the calendar view, tap **View** (located at the top of the screen).

3. Tap the desired view.

4. Then tap on an event to view.

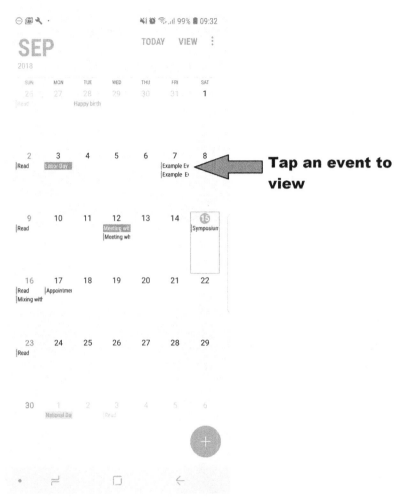

Editing, share or delete an event

1. From the Home screen, swipe up and tap on **Calendar**

2. To change the calendar view, tap **View** (located at the top of the screen). Tap the desired view.

3. Then tap on an event to view.

4. To delete an event, tap and hold the event and select **Delete**.

5. To share an event, tap and hold the event and select **Share**.

6. To edit an event, tap and hold the event and select **Edit**.

To customize the calendar app, from the Home screen, swipe up and tap **Calendar**

. Tap the menu icon ⋮ at the top of the screen. Tap **settings** and choose an option.

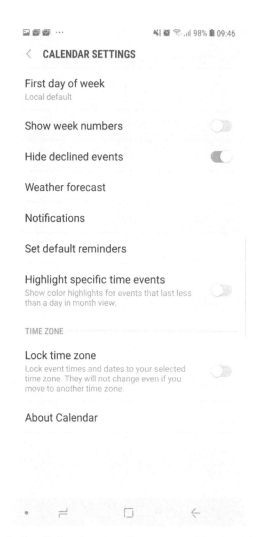

In addition, you can search the Calendar app for events. To do this, open the **Calendar** app and tap the menu icon ⋮ (located at the top of the screen). Then select **Search**. Enter a keyword or phrase and tap the lens icon 🔍 on the on-screen keyboard.

Google Calendar App

Google Calendar app helps you organize your schedules and tasks more conveniently and effectively. As at the time of writing this book, Google Calendar app has a more robust set of options than the Samsung Calendar app that comes with Note 9.

You can download Google Calendar app from Google Play store. In addition, if you have already added your Google account to your phone, the calendar events from this account should appear in the Google Calendar app.

If you have not added your Google account to your phone, you can do so by following these steps:

1. Swipe down from the top of the screen and select the settings icon ⚙ .

2. Tap **Cloud and accounts**.

3. Tap **Accounts**.

4. Tap **Add account.**

5. Tap **Google** and follow the prompts.

Creating an Event

1. From the Home screen, swipe up and tap on **Calendar** . If you are using the Calendar app for the first time, follow the on-screen instructions to set it up.

2. Tap the plus icon ⊕ at the lower right side of the screen and choose whether you want to create a **goal**, a **reminder**, or an **event.** In this example, **event** is selected.

3. To set the start and end date/time of the event, tap the on-screen date/time and adjust them accordingly. If the event is an all-day event, tap the status switch next to **All-day** to activate it. When you activate all-day, you would not be able to set a specific time for your event. To learn more about all-day event, see page 363.

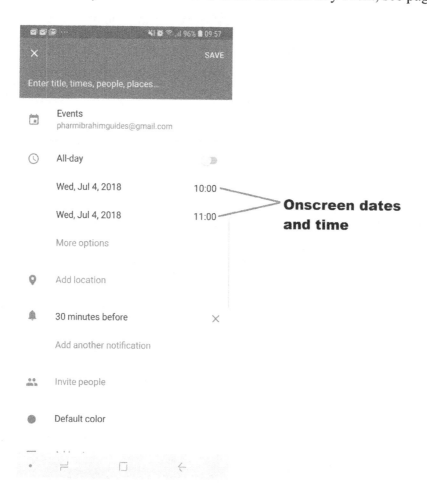

4. To enter a title for your event, tap "Enter title, times, people, places…" located at the top of the screen and enter a title. Tap **Done** to save the title. Fill in other details.

5. When you are done, tap **Save** (located at the top of the screen).

Your phone should give you a notification when the time for an event comes.

Creating a Reminder

1. From the home screen, swipe up and tap on **Calendar** 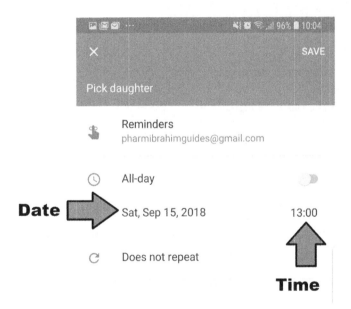 .

2. Tap the plus icon at the lower right side of the screen and choose **Reminder**.

3. Enter a title for your reminder or pick from the suggestions. Tap **Done** to save the title. If you don't want the reminder to be **all-day** (and you wish to set a specific time), tap the status switch next to **All-day** to deactivate it. When you deactivate all-day, you would be able to set a specific time.

4. Tap the date to adjust the date. Tap the time to adjust it.

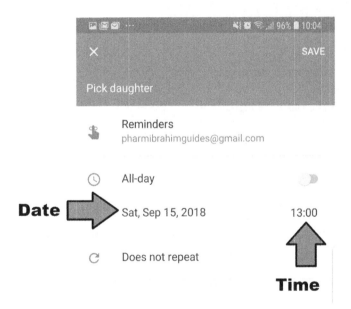

5. To choose when to repeat the reminder, tap **Does not repeat** and pick an option.

6. When you are done, tap **Save** (located at the top of the screen).

Creating a Goal

1. From the Home screen, swipe up and tap on **Calendar** .

2. Tap the plus icon at the lower right side of the screen and choose **Goal**.

3. Choose a goal and follow the onscreen instructions to complete the process.

4. To access more options, tap **More Options**. Tap the checkmark to save your goal.

5. Wait for the saving process to finish. If prompted, tap **Looks Good** if Google Calendar timing for your goal is OK, if not, tap **Adjust time**. Tap the pen icon , then tap the time and adjust it as you like. Tap **Save** (located at the top of the screen) to save the changes.

First time is tomorrow at 11:00
Does this time work for you?

ADJUST TIME   LOOKS GOOD

Understanding All-day Event

All-day event is a type of event that will take a lot of hours to be completed. For example, if an event will begin by 9 a.m. and finish by 6 p.m., this type of event should be categorized as an all-day event. This would make it easier to see all other schedules (like reminders) happening during this time on your calendar. If you were to schedule an event between 9 a.m. and 6 p.m. on your calendar (and you don't select it as all-day event), it will block off a lot of time on your calendar. It may also overshadow other concurrent events.

In the picture below, the event is supposed to be an all-day event, but I have refused to do so.

This is supposed to
be an all-day event

When I made the same event an all-day event, it becomes this (see below).

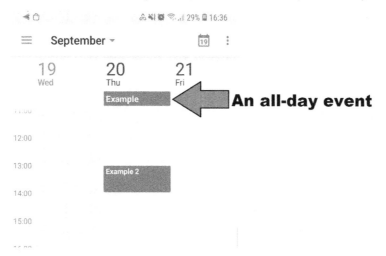

An all-day event

To make an event an all-day event, please go to step 3 under **Creating an Event** (see page 359).

Changing Calendar View

1. From the Home screen, swipe up and tap on **Calendar** .

2. To change the calendar view, tap the menu icon (located at the top of the screen).

3. Tap **Month**, **Week**, **3 Day** or **Day**.

Viewing an Event, Reminder or Goal

1. From the Home screen, swipe up and tap on **Calendar** .

2. To change the calendar view, tap the menu icon .

3. Select **Month**, **Week**, **3 Day** or **Day**.

4. Then tap on an event, reminder or goal to view.

Editing an Event, Reminder or Goal

1. Repeat steps 1 to 4 above.

2. Tap the pen icon and adjust what you want. Tap **Save** (located at the top of the screen) to save the changes.

Deleting an Event, Reminder or Goal

1. From the home screen, swipe up and tap on **Calendar** .

2. To change the calendar view, tap the menu icon (located at the top of the screen).

3. Select **Month**, **Week** or **Day**.

4. Then tap on an event, reminder or goal you want to delete.

5. Tap the menu icon and select **Delete**.

You can copy an event to another calendar. To do this, repeat steps 1 to 4 above and tap the menu icon . Then tap **Copy to...** and follow the prompts.

Inviting People to Your Events

If you have an upcoming event, you can invite people to it using the Google Calendar app. To do this:

1. From the Home screen, swipe up and tap on **Calendar** .

2. Tap the plus icon at the lower right side of the screen and choose **event**.

3. To set the start and end date/time of the event, tap onscreen date/time and adjust them accordingly. If the event is an all-day event, tap the status switch next to **All-day** to activate it. When you activate all-day, you would not be able to set a specific time. To learn more about all-day event, please see page 363.

4. To enter a title for your event, tap "Enter title, times, people, places…" located at the top of the screen and enter a title. Tap **Done** to save the title.

5. To invite people to your event, tap **Invite people** and type the name of those you are inviting. The list filters as you type. To select any suggested name, tap it. You can also enter email address if you don't have the contact of those you are inviting. In addition, if you have a Google group, you can enter the email address of the group to send invitations to the members of the group. Tap **Done.**

6. Fill in other details.

7. When you are done, tap **Save** (located at the top of the screen). If prompted, select **Send.**

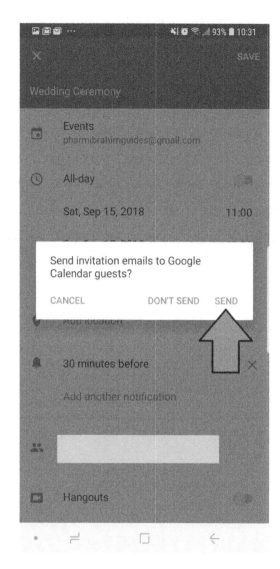

Generally, Google will send out email invitation to the invited guest/people after you save the event. The invitees will have the opportunity to respond to the request through their emails.

To see the people coming to your event, simply open Calendar app and tap on the event.

In addition, you can send invitation to thousands of people easily if you have Google group and you have these people (you want to invite) in your Google group. To create a group, visit groups.google.com

Controlling What You See in Your Calendar

You can choose what you see in your calendar. For example, if you don't want public holidays to appear in your calendar, you can prevent it. To do this:

1. From the Home screen, swipe up and tap **Calendar** .

2. Tap the menu icon 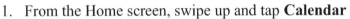 at the top of the screen.

3. Unselect those options you don't want to see in your calendar. For example, if you don't want your Reminder to populate your calendar, unselect it. Furthermore, if you don't want to see events from a Google account, you can use this method to unselect that Google account.

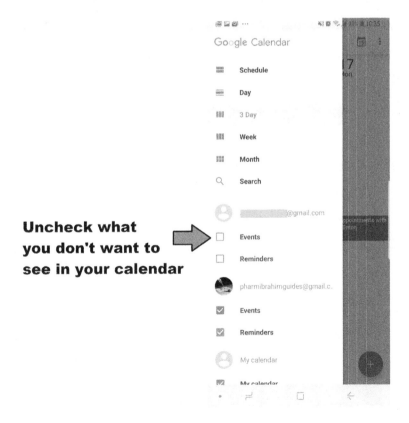

Uncheck what you don't want to see in your calendar

Managing Google Calendar App Settings

1. From the Home screen, swipe up and tap **Calendar** . Tap the menu icon at the top of the screen.

2. Scroll down and tap **Settings** (located at the bottom of the screen). Choose an option.

3. To access general settings, tap **General**. General settings allow you to manage settings like time zone, notifications, quick response etc.

4. To adjust event's notification, tap **Events.** Tap a default notification (for example, tap "30 minutes before") and choose another one. To add another notification, tap **Add another notification**. To pick another color for your event, tap **Color** and choose one.

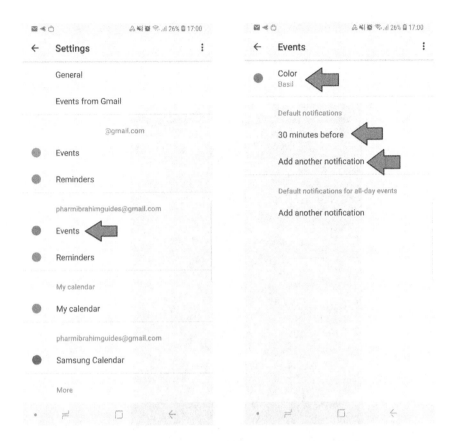

Using the Camera

Samsung Galaxy Note 9 comes with two rear-facing cameras, a front-facing camera and an LED flash. With these cameras, you can capture an image or record a video.

The memory capacity of the images taken may differ depending on the settings, shooting scenes and shooting conditions.

Number	Function
1.	Shooting mode: Camera app has many shooting modes and you would need to choose the shooting mode based on what you are doing. For example, if you are taking a picture of the waterfall, you

	can consider using panorama mode. Interestingly, your phone can also determine the ideal shooting mode for you whenever you access the camera. If you don't know which mode to choose, then make sure **Auto** is selected. To select another shooting mode, swipe left or right, or tap the name of the shooting mode.
2.	Flash light button
3.	Zoom button
4.	Front-facing/rear-facing camera switch
5.	Filters button
6.	Preview thumbnail tab
7.	Camera button
8.	Video button
9.	Camera settings
10.	Bixby Vision button. Tap this icon to get more information about the picture you are viewing. To learn more about Bixby vision, see page 224.
11.	Expand View/Full View

> **To Capture a photo**

1. While the phone is locked, double-press the Power Key (at the side of the phone) to launch the camera app. Please note that you may need to enable this feature. To do this, see page 374. Alternatively, from the app screen, tap **Camera.**

2. Aim the lens at the subject and make any necessary adjustments. To focus any part of the screen, tap that part of the screen.

3. To adjust the picture size, tap settings ⚙ and tap the **Picture size**. Please note that the picture size you pick may affect the memory size of your captured image.

4 Tap **front-facing/rear-facing icon** to switch between the front-facing and rear-facing cameras.

5. To zoom in, place two fingers on the screen and spread them apart. Do the reverse to zoom out.

6. Tap on **camera button** when you are done adjusting the settings.

★ You can choose to enable or disable **Review pictures**. To disable/enable **Review pictures,** tap the settings icon ⚙ while on the camera app, scroll down and tap the switch next to **Review pictures**. When the image review is enabled, you will see a preview of each photo immediately after you take a picture. This allows you to immediately delete the picture if you are not satisfied with it.

💡 To change the picture storage location to SD card, while on the camera app screen, tap the settings icon ⚙ . Then scroll down and tap **Storage Location.** Select **SD card** from the option that appears.

To open the Camera by quickly pressing the Power key twice:

1. Swipe down from the top of the screen and select the settings icon ⚙ .
2. Tap **Advanced features.**
3. Tap the switch next to **Quick launch camera** to activate it.

To customize camera settings:
1. From the app screen, tap **Camera.**

2. Tap the settings icon ⚙ .
3. Adjust the various settings as you like.

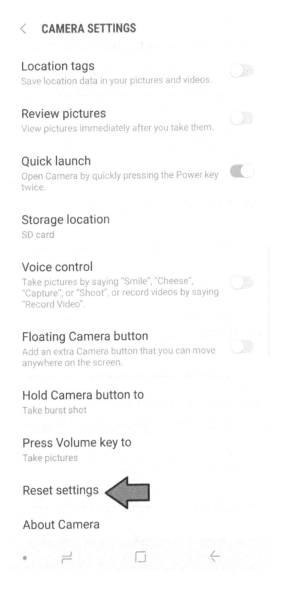

Camera settings consist of a lot of features and you may not need to touch some of these features. In fact, the default settings are enough for many users.

If someone adjusts the camera settings the way you don't like and you wish to restore the camera settings to factory settings, follow these steps. Tap the settings icon while on the camera app screen, scroll down and tap **Reset settings.** Tap **Reset** when prompted.

Recording a video

1. When the phone is locked, double-press the Power Key (at the side of the phone) to launch the camera app. Alternatively, from the Home screen, tap **Camera.**

2 Tap on the video button ⬤ to start recording.

3. To zoom in while recording, place two fingers on the screen and spread them apart. To zoom out, move the two fingers closer.

4. When done with the recording, tap the **video button** ⬛ again.

5. To view your recorded videos, go to **Gallery/Photos** app.

Editing Pictures

You can use your phone to edit pictures.

1. Swipe up the screen while on the Home screen and tap on **Gallery/Photos**.

2. Tap on the picture you want to edit.

3. Tap the **Edit icon** 🎨 and pick any editing tool(s).

Getting Productive With the Camera

Many people use the camera of their phone just to take pictures, but don't know that they can be more productive using their phone camera.

Interestingly, Galaxy Note 9 features a powerful camera that transforms the way you use a camera. In this part of the guide, we will be exploring ways we can be more productive with our phone camera.

Ways to be more productive with your phone camera are mentioned below:

- **Use your phone camera as a scanner for your documents**

You probably have many documents that are very important to you. Why don't you look for time to take the pictures of all these documents and save them to your phone or have them stored in the cloud. There are times that you would want to check something inside a document, but you are not at home. Saving your document on your phone should help you in a time like this. In addition, saving documents on your phone will save you time and stress because you have access to them on the go.

Top Android document scanners include **Microsoft Office Lens** and **Adobe Scan**. You can download these apps from Google Play store.

- **Take pictures of natural environment like waterfall and natural vegetation**

According to reports, looking at the pictures of natural environment like waterfalls and natural vegetations gives people pleasure and serves as coolness to one's eyes. In addition, it helps you appreciate the beautiful work of Almighty God.

- **Declutter your life**

Do you know that you can use the camera of your phone to declutter your life? You probably have many hand-written documents, business cards, to-do list etc. lying all over the places in your home. You can take the picture of these notes so that you can remove them from your house and give them to appropriate waste recycling companies. This will create more space in your house and give you visual ventilation.

I would advise you properly label the pictures of your hand-written documents, business cards, to-do list etc. to help you easily find them in the future. In addition, you can consider saving the pictures of your hand-written documents, business cards, to-do list etc. on *Evernote*. I suggest Evernote because it gives you the opportunity to search texts inside images.

- **Use your camera as a barcode and QR (quick response) code scanner**

Barcode and QR code are machine readable codes that are used to store information. Barcode is linear or one dimensional in nature. It basically looks like a cluster of parallel lines. On the other hand, QR code is two dimensional in nature. An example of a QR code is shown below. Interestingly, Samsung Galaxy Note 9 is capable of reading QR codes and barcodes using Bixby vision or barcode scanner apps. Many of us still take the long path of entering texts or links when we can get the same result by scanning barcode or QR code.

Example of a QR code

To use Bixby vision to scan a QR code:

1. Launch the phone camera and tap Bixby vision icon.

Bixby Vision Icon

An alternate way to access Bixby Vision is tapping on Bixby Vision icon ![icon] located on the applications screen.

2. Then scroll left and tap **QR code**.

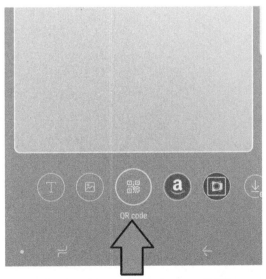

Scroll left and tap QR code

3. Aim your lens at the code and wait for response.

I noticed that Bixby vision can perform poorly when scanning barcodes and I would advise you install a third-party barcode scanner app. You can install a barcode scanner from Google Play store, simply search for *barcode scanner* or *QR and barcode scanner*.

- **Take the pictures of notes in meetings and lectures instead of writing them**

Taking the picture of notes after a meeting or a lecture allows you to listen during the meeting or lecture instead of writing notes.

- **Use your camera to take pictures of valuable information/documents in your life**

If you have any valuable piece of information that you can't afford to lose, use your camera to take its picture. That would serve as a backup in case of loss.

It is a good idea to back up your files/documents on cloud platforms like Dropbox, OneDrive or Google Drive.

Connectivity

Computer Connections

Your phone can be connected to a computer with a USB cable. This would enable you to transfer items such as audio, document and image files to your phone from your computer.

Warning: Do not disconnect the USB cable from a computer while the device is transferring or accessing data. This may result in data loss or damage to your phone.

Transferring content via USB

1. Connect your device to a computer with an appropriate USB cable (like the one that came with your phone).

2. When prompted to allow an access to phone data, tap **Allow.** If you don't choose Allow, your computer may not be able to access your phone.

3. Slide down from the top of the screen, tap the USB option (**USB for file transfer**) and tap it again.

4. Tap **Transfer Files** (if not selected).

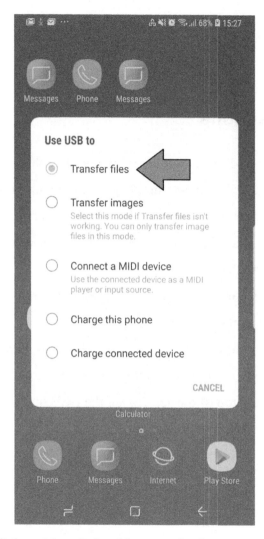

5. Your Samsung Galaxy Note 9 should appear in the same location where an external USB drive usually appear. For Windows users, this is typically under "This PC/Computer" menu.

6. Open your device drive to see the different folders present. Note that you may not be able to access the folders if your phone is locked.

7. To transfer files from your computer to your phone, locate the file you want to transfer on your computer. Then click, drag and drop the file into the corresponding folder on your Phone. Alternatively, if you are using a PC, right-

click on the file you want to send, select **Send to** and choose your phone from the options that appear.

8. Disconnect your phone just as you would disconnect an external memory drive. If you are using Windows 10, you may just remove the USB from the phone when you are done with the transfer. You may not need to click any disconnect icon before you remove your phone if you are using Windows 10.

After the transfer, your transferred files should appear under the corresponding content library on your device. To view any of the transferred files:

From the Home screen, swipe up and tap **Samsung folder** > **My Files**. Then tap an appropriate category to view the transferred files or folders.

In addition, you may consider installing **Files Go by Google** from Google Play store to manage your files better.

Note that your phone will only recognize the file you transferred if the file is a supported file type.

If you do factory reset to your phone, you may need to re-transfer the files again (unless you have them stored on a cloud storage like Dropbox).

Wi-Fi

Using your phone, you can connect to the internet or other network devices anywhere an access point or wireless hotspot is available.

To activate the Wi-Fi feature and connect to a network:

1. Swipe down from the top of the screen.

2. Tap and hold the **Wi-Fi** icon.

3. Tap the switch next to Wi-Fi to turn it on.

4. Your device then automatically scans for available networks and displays them.

5. Select a network and enter a password for the network (if needed). You may also manually add a network. To manually add a network, scroll down (if necessary) and tap **Add network**. Then follow the on-screen instructions.

6. To turn Wi-Fi off, swipe down from the top of the screen and tap the Wi-Fi icon
 .

- The Wi-Fi feature running in the background will consume battery. To save battery, put it off whenever you are not using it.

- The Wi-Fi may not connect to a network if the network signal is not good.

- When Wi-Fi is connected, active and communicating with a wireless Access Point, Wi-Fi active icon is displayed on the Status bar.

Wi-Fi Active Icon

Mobile Data

Using your phone, you can connect to the internet or other network devices using the Mobile Data.

To enable mobile data:

1. Swipe down from the top of the screen.

2. Tap and hold the **Mobile data** icon to access mobile data settings.

3. Tap the switch next to **Mobile Data** to turn it on.

Please note that you may incur charges when using mobile data.

Using Your Phone as a Hotspot

If your network provider supports it, you can use this feature to share your mobile network with friends.

1. Swipe down from the top of the screen and select the settings icon ⚙ . Tap **Connections** tab.

2. Tap **Mobile Hotspot and Tethering**.

3. Tap **Mobile hotspot**. If prompted to enable or disable Wi-Fi sharing, you can choose to disable Wi-Fi sharing. Wi-Fi sharing allows you to share your Wi-Fi connections with other devices, while mobile hotspot shares your mobile data with other devices. Please before you share a Wi-Fi connection with other devices, please ensures that you are not breaking any terms and conditions.

4. Next to Mobile Hotspot, tap **On**. Please note that Wi-Fi would need to be turned off for you to turn on mobile hotspot.

5. To set the password and enable password protection, tap the menu icon ⋮ (located at the top of the screen) and tap **Configure Mobile Hotspot.** Enter a name for the network (this is the name that other devices searching for the network will see).

6. If you don't want your device (hotspot to be visible), tap **Hide my device**.

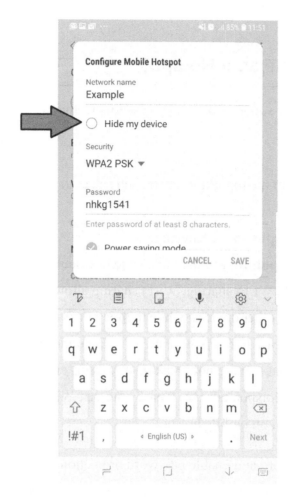

7. Scroll down and tap **Password**. Then enter a password for the network and tap **Save**.

8. After enabling the mobile hotspot, your friends should be able to connect to it just like they connect to wireless networks.

You can choose who connects to your mobile hotspot by creating the **Allowed Device** list. To do this:

1. Follow steps 1 to 4 above.

2. Tap the menu icon ⋮ > **Allowed devices**, then tap **Add** to enter the device name and MAC address. The MAC address of many smart gadgets is found under **Wi-Fi settings** or **Wi-Fi Advanced settings.**

3. Tap **Add** to add the device.

4. Tap the status switch next to **Allowed devices only** to make sure only the allowed devices can connect to your mobile hotspot.

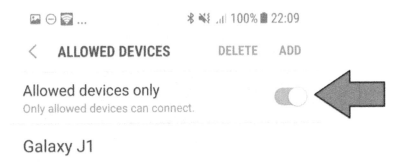

5. To delete an allowed device, tap and hold the device and select **DELETE.**

In addition, you can automatically turn off Mobile hotspot if there are no connected devices. To do this, follow step 1 above. Then tap the menu icon ⋮ > **Timeout settings** and select a time.

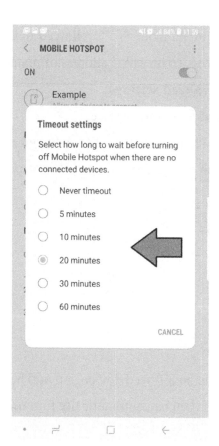

Access More by Using Bluetooth

Bluetooth option allows you to connect to another Bluetooth device within range.

If there are obstacles, the operating distance of the Bluetooth may be reduced. The Bluetooth communication range is usually approximately 30 feet.

To use the Bluetooth feature:

1. Swipe down from the top of the screen.

2. Tap and hold the **Bluetooth** icon .

3. Then tap the status switch below the **Bluetooth**.

4. Bluetooth automatically scans for nearby Bluetooth devices and displays them. Please make sure the Bluetooth of the device you are connecting with is turned on and discoverable.

5. Tap a device to connect with and follow the prompts to finish the connection. You may need to enter a pairing code.

6. When Bluetooth is enabled, the **Bluetooth icon** would appear on the Status bar. Pairing between two Bluetooth devices should be a one-time process. Once two devices are paired, the devices may continue to recognize this connection and you may not need to re-enter a passcode.

7. To turn Bluetooth off, swipe down from the top of the screen, tap **Bluetooth** . The Bluetooth would appear gray when you turn it off (see the picture below).

Unpairing a Paired Device

1. Swipe down from the top of the screen.

2. Tap and hold the **Bluetooth** icon.

3. Then next to **Bluetooth**, select **on** (if not already turned on).

4. Tap the settings icon next to the paired device and tap **Unpair** to delete the paired device.

💡 Once you have paired your device to another device, you can rename the paired device to make it easier to recognize. To do this, follow steps 1 to 3 above and tap the settings icon ⚙ next to the previously paired device. Then tap **Rename**. Enter a new name and tap **Rename**.

Location Services

Enabling location service allows apps to serve you content-related services.

To activate location services:

1. Swipe down from the top of the screen and select the settings icon ⚙ . Tap **Connection.**
2. Tap **Location.**
3. Under **Location**, tap the switch to select **on.**
4. To put it off, tap the switch again.

💡 If you want your phone to use the combination of Wi-Fi, GPS and mobile networks to estimate your location, tap **Location Method**, then tap **High accuracy.**

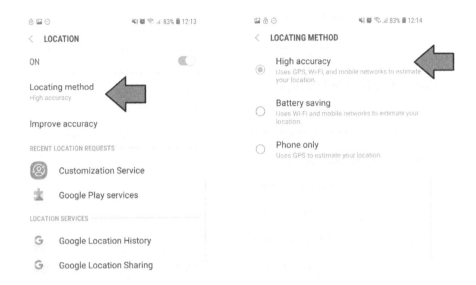

Find My Mobile

You can use this feature to locate your phone if lost.

★ You must sign up for a Samsung account and enable location service (as explained above) to use **Find My Mobile**.

To add Samsung account (if you have not done so before):

1. Swipe down from the top of the screen and select the settings icon ⚙.

2. Tap **Cloud and accounts**.

3. Tap **Account**.

4. Tap **Add account**.

5. Tap **Samsung Account**. Then enter your Samsung account information.

6. Or tap **Create Account** and follow the prompts.

Please note that if you have already added Samsung account, you can skip these steps.

To activate Find My Mobile Feature:

1. Swipe down from the top of the screen and select the settings icon .

2. Tap **Biometrics and security**.

3. Scroll down and tap **Find My Mobile**.

4. If required, enter your Samsung account password and tap **Sign In.** If you don't have a Samsung account, create one.

5. Make sure that the status switches next to **Remote Controls, Google Location Service** and **Send Last Location** are turned on.

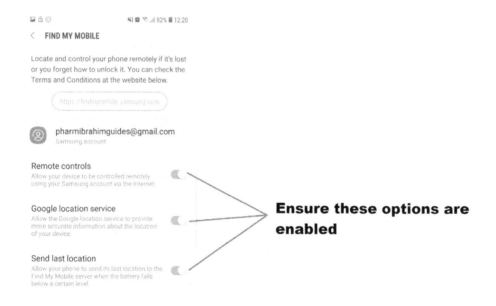

To find your lost phone:

1. Open a web browser and go to **findmymobile.samsung.com**

2. Tap **Sign In.**

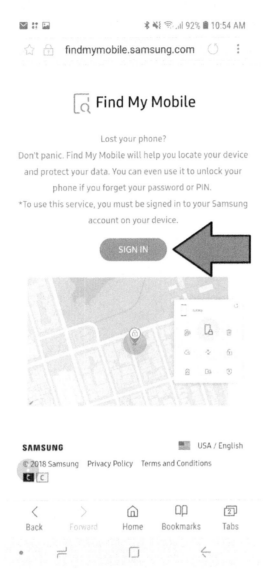

3. Enter the email address associated with your Samsung account into the email field and enter your password. Tap **Sign In.**

4. If you have more than one Samsung phone, you may need to select your Samsung

Galaxy Note 9 (if it is not currently displayed). To do this, tap the menu icon ≡ next to the current device name and select your device name.

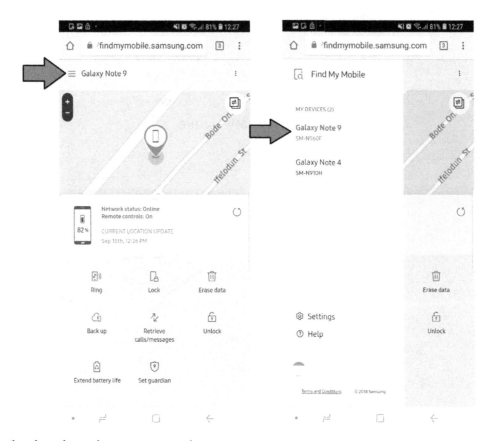

5. Tap the dropdown icon to access the map.

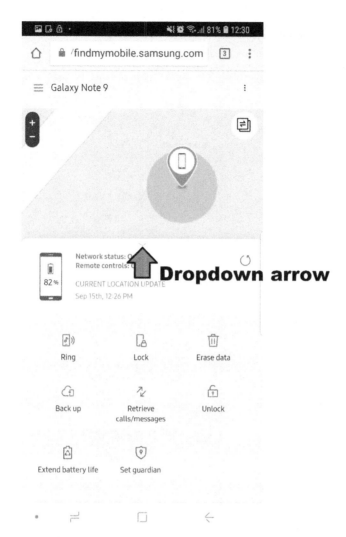

6. To close the map, tap the V-shaped icon.

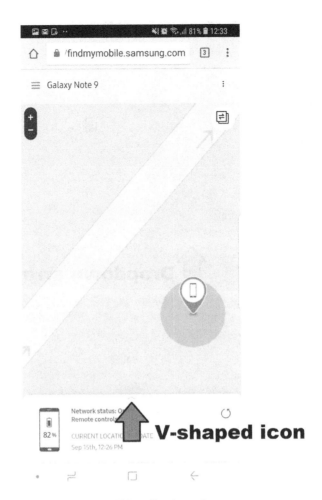

The current location of your phone will be displayed on a map.

You can use the options on this website to **ring your device, lock your device, back up your device, extend battery life, set guardian, retrieve calls/messages, and wipe/erase your device**.

You can use **Find My Device** to unlock your device when you forget your log in information. To do this, follow steps 1-4 above and tap **Unlock**. Then enter your Samsung account password.

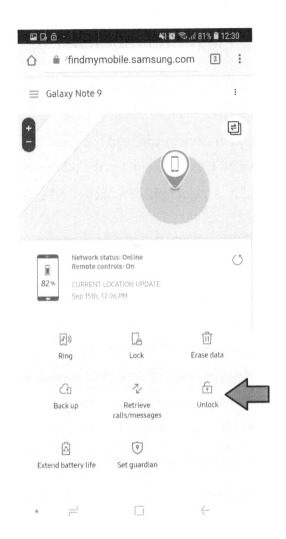

Please note that your phone may need to be connected to a wireless or mobile network to be able to use the **Find My Mobile** feature to manage your phone. However, you may still be able to know the last known location of your phone even if not connected.

Using the NFC (Near Field Communication)

This is a technology like Bluetooth and Wi-Fi. It utilizes electromagnetic radio frequency. Devices using NFC may be passive or active. A passive device is not powered by a battery but contains information that other devices can read but does not read any information itself. An example of a passive NFC is NFC tag. On the other hand, an active NFC device can read information and send it. An example of an active NFC device is your Samsung Galaxy Note 9

You can use NFC feature to send files from your phone to other NFC supported devices.

To turn on and use NFC:

1. Swipe down from the top of the screen using two fingers, then tap and hold the

   NFC icon ⓝ for two seconds. Please note that you may need to swipe to the right to access more quick settings options before you can see the **NFC** icon.

2. Under **NFC and payment,** tap the switch to turn it on. Also make sure the status switch next to **Android Beam** is turned on.

3. To use NFC to send a file to another device, ensure both devices involved have their NFC turned on. Then open the file you wish to send and tap **Share**. Scroll down (if needed) and tap **Android Beam**. Hold your mobile phone and the receiving device back to back. Then tap the screen to send the file.

It may not be very effective in sending large files because it may be slow.

Using NFC to make payments

In recent times, NFC is finding more usage in payment system.

Making payments with NFC:

1. Follow steps 1 and 2 above (under **To turn on and use NFC**).
2. Touch the back of your device to the NFC card reader.

Usually, after you have enabled NFC payments on your phone, you should be able to make payments for items by tapping your phone against a participating store's NFC reader.

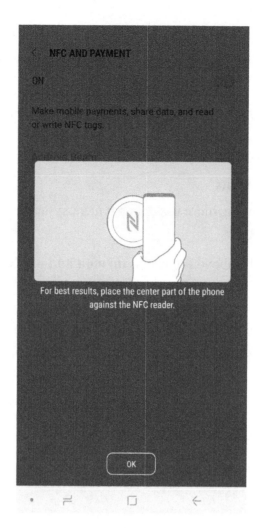

For best results, place the center part of the phone against the NFC reader.

You can select the default payment application you want to use for making purchases on your device if you have more than one payment method installed. To do this, when on **NFC and payment** screen, tap **Tap and pay** and tap **PAYMENT** (located at the top of the screen). Then select a default payment app.

Settings

Settings menu give you the opportunity to customize your device as you like.

To access the settings menu

1. Swipe down from the top of the screen and select the settings icon ⚙.
2. Alternatively, swipe up from the Home screen and tap **Settings**.
3. Tap a setting category.

Search for Settings

It is advisable to use the searching feature when you are not sure exactly where to find a certain setting.

1. Swipe down from the top of the screen and select the settings icon ⚙.
2. Tap Search bar.
3. Enter a word or words in the Search field. The list filters as you write.
4. Tap an option (make sure you select the best match).

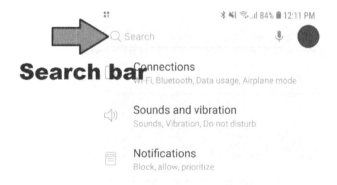

💡 There is a tip to getting what you want from your device. From time to time, you would want to customize your phone in a special way. All you need to do to get started is to open the settings as described above. Then tap the search bar and enter a search word or phrase corresponding to what you want to do.

What You Must Know About Samsung Galaxy Note 9

How to Find Your Phone When lost

As a human being, it is not impossible that you misplace your phone. If someone else (a thief) has not taken custody of it, there are steps to follow to find it. These steps have been discussed at length in the preceding section; please refer to page 391-396 for details.

Staying Productive While Using Your Samsung Galaxy Note 9

Smartphones are cool things to have, but if you are not careful, they might get you entangled. Many people spend less time with friends and family because of their phone. They enjoy pressing their phones all the time even if it adds little or no meaning to their lives.

The truth is that if you want to stay productive, you must know when to drop your phone and do things that are more important to you. You must know when to switch off your phone or avoid using the internet. I have noticed that it is easier said than done. For most of us, it is difficult to drop our phones (and avoid online chats) to attend to other important things. What I have personally observed is that many of us need an outside help. One of the beautiful things we need is a good software (application) to make us accountable and prevent internet/app access when we are tempted.

Cold Turkey app is one of the apps out there that can help you block apps on your phone (for a specified time) so that you can concentrate on other things. You can download **Cold Turkey** app on Google Play store.

In addition, if you are looking for an accountable app that will enable you to know how you spend your time, you can try RescueTime Time Management app. This app will let you know how you spend your time on your phone. It will also let you know how productive you are. You can learn more and download **RescueTime Time Management** app from Google Play store.

Finally, one application that has personally helped me in my life is Freedom application. This application has helped me to avoid internet or apps when I need to do other important things. Unfortunately, as at the time of writing this guide, this app is not available on Android. However, it is available on Windows and iOS. You can learn more about Freedom at **https://freedom.to**

How to Reduce Data Usage on Samsung Galaxy Note 9

If you realize that you use more data than normal, there are steps to follow to reduce your data consumption.

1. The first thing is to make sure that you update apps on Wi-Fi only. To do this:
    a. Swipe up from the Home screen and tap **Play Store**.
    b. Tap the menu icon.

c. Tap **Settings**.
    d. Tap **Auto-update apps** and select **Auto-update apps over Wi-Fi only** or **Do not auto-update apps.**
2. Consider using a data friendly browser: A browser like **Opera Mini** gives you the opportunity to save data through their **data saving** feature. You can also control

the picture quality of webpages when you are using Opera Mini browser and thereby saving data. To download Opera Mini, please visit Google Play store.

3. Enable Data saver: To do this, from a Home screen, tap the settings icon ⚙ . Tap **Connections**. Tap **Data usage** and tap **Data saver**. Tap the status switch next to **Data saver**.

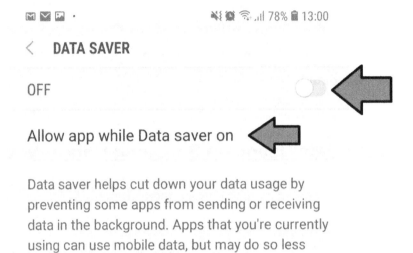

To control the number of apps that have unrestricted access to your data, tap **Allow app while Data saver on** (see the picture above).

4. Use the **Datally** app. This app allows you to save and control the use of your data. To download Datally, please visit Google Play store.

Solution to Non-Responding Apps

Sometimes, an app may start misbehaving and may even refuse to close. The first thing you can do in a situation like this is to tap on the recent button . This gives you access to all opened/running apps on your phone. Locate this app and tap **X** icon to close it. Try launching the app again.

If it keeps misbehaving after closing it or it refuses to close, then you may try these steps:

1. Swipe down from the top of the screen and select the settings icon .
2. Tap **Apps**.
3. Then tap on the misbehaving application from the list of applications.
4. Select **FORCE STOP**. This will stop the app from carrying out any process on your phone. To enable the app again, just launch the app.

Please restart your device if stopping an app causes your device to stop working correctly. *In addition, force stopping an app may cause error(s).*

How to Conserve Samsung Galaxy Note 9's Battery Life

You may notice that you have to charge Samsung Galaxy Note 9 twice in 24 hours to keep it running. There are steps to follow to ensure that your phone serves you throughout the day with just a single charge.

1. **Reduce the screen brightness and turn off the automatic brightness:** I have realized over time that high screen brightness level consumes a lot of energy. There is usually a substantial difference between using a phone with a maximum brightness level and using it with a moderate brightness level. As a rule, don't use your phone with a maximum brightness level unless you can't see what is on the

screen clearly. For example, if you are outdoor. Make sure you reduce it immediately when it is no more needed.

To reduce the screen brightness, swipe down from the top of the screen using two fingers. Then use the small circle on the slider to adjust the brightness level.

To manage Auto brightness, tap the **dropdown arrow** ⌄ next to the brightness slider and tap the switch next to **Auto brightness**.

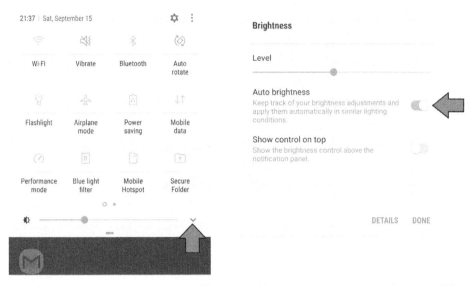

2. **Shorten the Screen timeout:** if you really want to save your battery life, you must try to shorten the screen timeout. Reducing how long your phone would stay lit up after you finish interacting with it will help you to save your battery. To manage the screen timeout setting:

    a. Swipe down from the top of the screen and select the settings icon .

    b. Tap **Display**.

    c. Scroll down and tap on **Screen Timeout**. Then choose an option.

‹   **SCREEN TIMEOUT**

◯   15 seconds

◉   30 seconds

◯   1 minute   **Choose an option**

◯   2 minutes

◯   5 minutes

◯   10 minutes

3. **Turn off Wi-Fi, Mobile Hotspot and Bluetooth:** when you are not using Wi-Fi. Mobile hotspot or Bluetooth, please always remember to put them off. These features really consume energy and they are better off when not in use.

4. **Reduce number of notifications:** there are two benefits of doing this. The first is that there will be less distractions and the second benefit is that it conserves energy. Limit yourself to those notifications that are important to you. To manage notification setting for an app:

   a. Swipe down from the top of the screen and select the settings icon .

   b. Tap **Apps**.

   c. Tap an app.

   d. Tap on **Notifications** to configure the notifications setting for the chosen app. To disable the notification for an app, tap the indicator switch next to **On.**

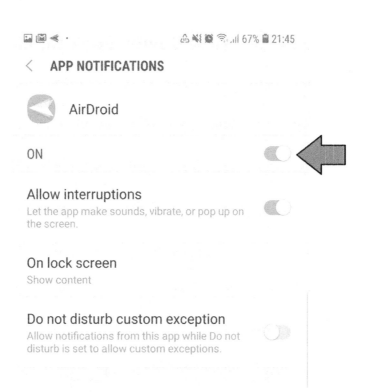

5. **Close all unnecessary apps:** the truth is that any app you access consumes part of the limited battery energy. It is important to close any app you are not using from time to time. To access all apps currently running on your phone, tap on the recent button ![icon], then tap **X** icon next to the application you want to close. Alternatively, swipe left or right to close an app. You can also put apps to sleep. To learn how to do this, go to page 18.

6. **Use the correct charger:** using a wrong charger can endanger the health of your phone/battery and it is better to avoid such practices.

7. **Consider switching off your phone:** if you are not going to use your phone for an extended period, you may consider switching it off.

What to Do if You Forget Your Device Lock Screen Password/Pin

1. Open a web browser and go to **findmymobile.samsung.com**
2. Tap **Sign In.**

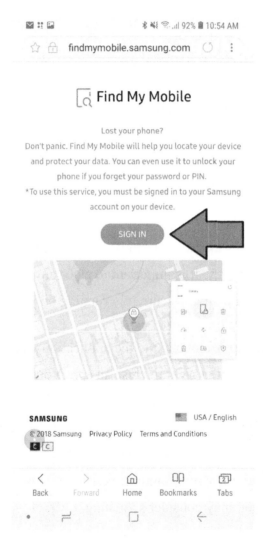

3. Enter the email address associated with your Samsung account into the email field and enter your password. Tap **Sign In.**

4. If you have more than one Samsung phone, you may need to select your Samsung

Galaxy Note 9 (if it is not currently displayed). To do this, tap the menu icon ☰ next to the current device name and select your device name.

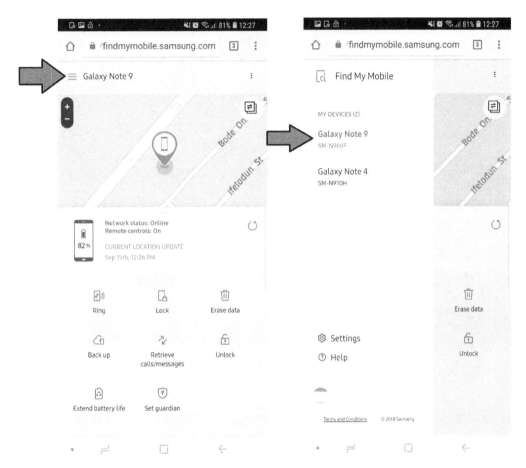

5. Tap **Unlock** and enter your Samsung account password.

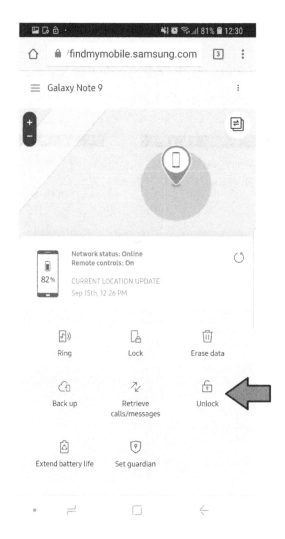

Your phone may need to be connected to a wireless or mobile network to be able to use the **Find My Mobile** feature to unlock your phone.

In addition, please note that if you have disabled **Remote Controls**, you would need to activate it before you can use the method above. To do this:

1. Swipe down from the top of the screen and select the settings icon ⚙.
2. Tap **Biometrics and security**.
3. Tap **Find My Mobile**.

4. Enter your Samsung account information and tap **Sign In.** If you don't have a Samsung account, create one.

5. Make sure that the status switches next to **Remote Controls**, **Google Location Service** and **Send Last Location** are turned on.

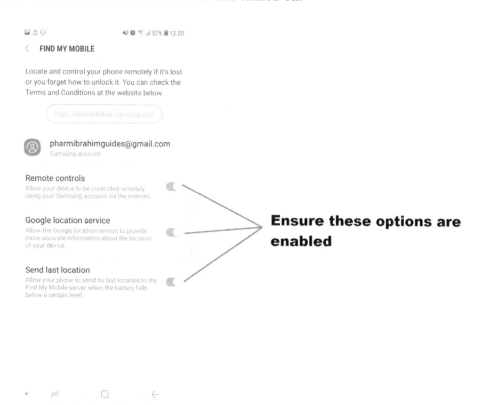

How to Take Screenshot on Your Device

Another task you can perform on your device is taking a screenshot.

To take a screenshot with your device, please follow the instructions below:

Method 1

Press and hold the volume down key and the power key simultaneously until you hear a small sound/vibration. You can view captured images in Gallery.

Method 2

You can also capture screenshots by swiping your hand to the left or right across the screen. To be able to use this method, you have to enable it. To do this:

1. Swipe down from the top of the screen and select the settings icon .

2. Scroll down and tap **Advanced features**.

3. Tap **Palm swipe to capture** and tap the status switch to activate it.

To capture a screenshot when this feature is enabled, just swipe the edge of your hand across more than half of the screen.

The Smart Capture

You can capture a screen and the scrollable area. In addition, you can immediately crop and share the captured screen. This feature is usually enabled by default, but if you want to check whether it is enabled or not, please follow the instructions below:

1. Swipe down from the top of the screen and select the settings icon .

2. Scroll down and tap **Advanced features**.

3. Tap **Smart capture** and tap the status switch to activate it.

Thereafter, press and hold the volume down key and the power key simultaneously to take a screenshot. Then tap on any of the options below:

Bixby Vision: Tap this icon to get more information about the screenshot you have captured. To learn more about Bixby Vision, see page 224.

Scroll Capture: Use this to capture the hidden parts of the screen. When you tap this icon, the screen would automatically scroll down and more contents would be captured. To capture more screens, tap this icon again.

Draw: Use this option to annotate the screenshot.

Crop: Use this to crop a portion from the screenshot.

Share: Use this to share the screenshot.

Extras

What You Must Know Before Selling or Giving Away Your Samsung Galaxy Note 9

A time would probably come when you may need to give away or sell your Samsung Galaxy Note 9. There are few things you must know before this time comes.

Some time ago, BBC reported that Avast (an antivirus giant) was able to use publicly available forensic security tools to extract naked selfies from second-hand phones bought on eBay. Other extracted data were emails, text messages and Google searches.

It is usual for many users to perform factory resets before selling their phones. The truth is that with the advent of sophisticated software, factory reset is no more enough. In fact, you have to go a step further.

So, what can you do to save your privacy? The simple answer is to go a step further by always encrypting your files. You should encrypt all your data before performing factory reset when you are considering selling or giving away your Phone.

However, you must know that encrypting your device before doing the factory reset may not give 100% protection to your privacy. Who knows if programmers will develop a software that would be a step ahead of that in the nearest future? The best way to completely protect your privacy is to destroy your phone when you don't need it again. But as you know, this is not feasible all the time and may not be advisable.

Finally, encrypting your phone before performing factory reset is an efficient way of protecting your privacy. At least it makes it much more difficult for people to retrieve your files.

Interestingly, Samsung Galaxy Note 9 automatically encrypts data stored on it. However, you would need to encrypt data stored on memory card yourself. To do that:

- From the Home screen, swipe up from the bottom of the screen and tap **Settings**.
- Tap **Biometrics and security > Encrypt SD card**.

- Read the onscreen information and if you are satisfied with it, tap **Encrypt SD card**.

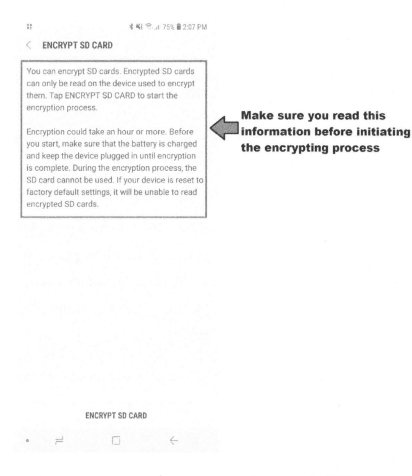

Make sure you read this information before initiating the encrypting process

When you encrypt your memory card, you may need a numeric PIN or password to decrypt your SD card when you first access it after switching on your device.

💡 You would need to reset your phone to factory settings before selling or giving it away. This would ensure you delete all your data on it. If necessary, make sure you back up your files before perfoming factory reset.

To remove all the data on your phone:

1. Swipe down from the top of the screen and select the settings icon ⚙ .
2. Scroll down and tap **General management**.

3. Tap **Reset**.

4. Tap **Factory data reset**.

5. Scroll down (if needed) and tap **Reset**.

Travelling with Your Phone—What to Know

While travelling abroad with your Samsung Galaxy Note 9, there are few things to know. These things are discussed below.

1. Unlock your phone and plan to get a local SIM card

If you are travelling abroad, it is important you consider unlocking your phone to use foreign SIM cards on your phone. Generally, you can unlock your phone by contacting your network service provider. If your phone is already unlocked, then have a clear plan to get a local SIM card when you get to the foreign land. Generally, using a local SIM card for your calls will save your money than roaming.

If you are unable to unlock your phone and you want to stay several months abroad, consider buying a cheap unlocked phone.

2. Get to know about roaming

If you are not planning to unlock your phone or get a local SIM card, then I would advise that you know about roaming plans. You can easily do this by contacting your network service provider.

3. Set up a lock screen

It is important to set up a lock screen while going abroad. This would save you a lot of stress if you misplace the phone. Security in some places in the world is bad and your phone can easily be snatched from you. Even if your phone is not stolen, you can misplace your phone while moving from one place to another.

If you have set up a screen lock, you can be sure that it would be extremely hard (if not impossible) for people to access your data from the lost phone. To know how to set up a lock screen, see page 142. I would advise you to use a lock screen password (if you can) for your device. A lock screen password appears more secured than pattern or PIN.

💡 If you mistakenly misplace your phone, you may locate it by following the steps on page 391 to 396.

4. Get a power bank (USB Battery Pack)

Charging your phone might not be easy while abroad. I would advise you consider getting a power bank to charge your phone. You can get a cheap and reliable power bank from Amazon.

5. Monitor and save your data

Data are quite expensive in some countries of the world. I would advise you monitor and save data as much as you can. To know how to save data on your phone, see page 403.

6. Be careful when using Wireless network

Using a wireless network in a foreign country needs extra care. There are some countries that are notorious for hacking. I would advise you research about any country you are visiting to know how to prepare for it. To learn how to stay secured when connected to wireless, see page 422.

7. Get familiar with Google Translate

If the country you are visiting does not speak your language, then you need someone or something to help you with language translation. Interestingly, Google Translate might provide some help in this regard. To start using Google Translate, visit **https://translate.google.com**

8. Get familiar with the Google Map application

Google Map is one of the best map applications in the world. You can easily know the route to your destination using this app. I would advise you familiarize yourself with Google Map before traveling. This application can save you a lot of stress and time. You can download **Google Map** from Google Play store.

Getting an antivirus for your phone -- is it necessary?

Many people may not really take the issue of antivirus seriously because they think that virus software target PCs much more than phones. The truth is that things are changing every now and then. The best thing you can do is to always keep a guard.
Interestingly, there is a device protection on Samsung Galaxy Note 9, to access this protection:

- From the Home screen, swipe up from the bottom of the screen and tap **Settings**.
- Tap **Device Maintenance**
- Tap **Device security** (located at the lower right part of the screen).
- Read the terms and conditions and select **Agree** to continue.
- To scan your phone, tap on **Scan Phone**.

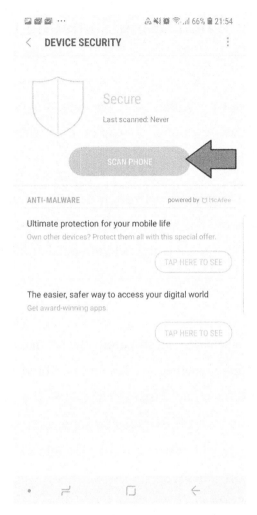

In addition, there are many reputable free antiviruses on Google Play store. My favorite antiviruses are AVG, Lookout and Norton Antiviruses. You may check Google Play Store to download any of these.

The best way to protect yourself from a virus attack is being proactive. For example, I don't expect you to click the links in an unsolicited email. So, having many antiviruses on your phone may not help if you are not prudent in your actions.

Safety Precautions When Using Samsung Galaxy Note 9 on Wi-Fi

With many free Wi-Fi hotspots, it is likely that you are going to find yourself using Wi-Fi more on your phone. There are few things to keep in mind when using Wi-Fi.

1. **Confirm the Network Name**

Hackers sometimes set up a fake Wi-Fi network in order to tap into the information of unwitting public users. To avoid this, make sure you are sure of the name of the network you are connecting to. You may ask any trusted individual around you if you doubt the name of a network.

2. **Connect to a Secured Site**

Whenever you are sending a sensitive information, always make sure that the site is a secured website. You can know whether a website is a secured site or not by checking whether the *url* address of the website starts with **HTTPS.** If it starts with https, then it should be a secured site. However, please note that some websites might start with https but are still unsecured. Anyway, browsing apps like Google Chrome would usually warn you when visiting websites like these.

3. **Run an Antivirus Software**

As earlier mentioned, using an antivirus is very crucial in today's world. You may consider installing a genuine antivirus. There are many of them on Google Play store.

4. **Get a Virtual Private Network (VPN)**

It is highly important you use a virtual private network when using a public wireless network. There are both free and paid VPN providers. My favorite is **Hotspot Shield VPN.** It is available on Google Play store. They offer both free and paid versions. You may also check out other VPN apps to pick the best.

5. Avoid Automatic Connection

Make sure your Wi-Fi is off when not using it to avoid your phone automatically connecting to an open network. Turning your Wi-Fi off when not using it will also save your battery.

I am Having a Dwindling Love for my Samsung Galaxy Note 9; What Should I Do?

It is possible that after buying Samsung Galaxy Note 9, you realize that it performs below your expectation. It is likely that you dislike your phone because of its hardware or software issue. Generally, the hardware has to do with the design, the phone make up, the weight of the phone etc. While the software has to do with the OS and applications.

If your love for Samsung Galaxy Note 9 is reducing because of the software, there is a way out. You can take your time to look for beneficial apps to install on your device.

If your love for Samsung Galaxy Note 9 is reducing because of the hardware, then you could consider learning how to live with it (you may have to force yourself to love it), giving it away or selling it. If you are considering selling your phone or giving it away, then make sure you read the article on page 416 to 418.

TROUBLESHOOTING

If the touch screen responds slowly or improperly or your phone is not responding, try the following:

- Remove any protective covers (screen protector) from the touch screen.
- Ensure that your hands are clean and dry when tapping. In addition, ensure that the screen of your phone is not wet. If wet, use a soft dry towel to clean it.
- Press the power button once to lock the screen and press it again to unlock the screen and enter a PIN/password/pattern if required.
- Restart your device.

Your phone doesn't charge

- Make sure you are using an appropriate Samsung charger to charge your phone.
- If the Samsung Galaxy Note 9 does not indicate that it is charging, unplug the power adapter and restart your device.
- Make sure you use the USB cable that came with the Samsung Galaxy Note 9 or anyone that has similar specs.

Your device is hot to the touch

When you use applications that require more power or use applications on your device for an extended period, your phone may be a bit hot. This is normal and it should not have much effect on its performance. You may just allow your phone to rest for some time or close some applications.

Your phone freezes or has fatal error

If your phone freezes or it is unresponsive, press and hold the Power key and the Volume Down key simultaneously until the screen goes off, then wait for it to restart automatically. Please note that you may need to press the Power key and the Volume Down key simultaneously for more than 5 seconds before the phone will restart.

Phone does not connect to Wi-Fi

Make sure you don't have limited network connectivity in that area. If your network signal is good and you still cannot connect, you may perform any of these actions.

- Make sure your Airplane Mode is off.
- Try restarting the Wi-Fi.
- Move closer to your router and scan for the available networks. If the network still does not show up, you may add the network manually.
- Restart your router and modem. Unplug the modem and router for few minutes and plug the modem in, then the router.
- Try restarting your phone.

Phone screen color is appearing somehow

- Check if you have not mistakenly turned on blue light filter. To do this, go to

   Settings 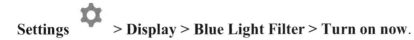 **> Display > Blue Light Filter > Turn on now**.

Another Bluetooth device is not located

- Ensure Bluetooth feature is activated on your phone and the device you want to connect to.
- Ensure that your phone and the other Bluetooth device are within the maximum Bluetooth range (usually approximately 30 feet).

A connection is not established when you connect your phone to a PC using USB cable

- Ensure that the USB cable you are using is compatible with your device and can transfer files.
- Ensure the USB port on your computer/phone is working properly.
- Ensure that you have the proper drivers installed and updated on your PC.

Audio quality is poor during a call

- Ensure that the network signal is strong. When you are in an area with a weak or poor reception, you may lose reception. Try moving to another area and try again.

Safety precautions

A. To prevent electric shock, fire and explosion

1. Do not use damaged power cords or plugs or loose electrical sockets.
2. Do not touch the power cord with a wet hand.
3. Do not bend or damage the power cord.
4. Do not short-circuit the charger.
5. Do not use your phone during thunderstorm.
6. Do not dispose your phone by putting it in fire.

B. Follow all safety warnings and regulations when using your device in restricted areas.

C. Comply with all safety warnings and regulations regarding mobile device usage while operating a vehicle.

D. Proper care and use of your phone

1. Do not use or store your phone in hot or cold areas. It is recommended to use your device in an area with a temperature from 5^0C to 35^0C.
2. Do not put your phone near magnetic fields.
3. Do not use camera flash close to eyes of people or pets because it can cause temporary loss of vision or damage the eyes.
4. When speaking on the phone, speak directly into the mouthpiece.
5. Avoid disturbing others when using your phone in public.
6. Keep your phone away from children because they may mistakenly damage it as it may look like a toy to them.

Just Before You Go (Please Read!)

Although I have put in tremendous effort in writing this guide,

I am confident that I have not said it all.

I have no doubt believing that I have not written everything possible about Samsung

Galaxy Note 9

So, I want you to do me a favor.

If you would like to know how to perform a task that is not included in this guide, please

let me know by sending me an email at **pharmibrahimguides@gmail.com**. I will try as

much as possible to reply you as soon as I can.

You may also visit my author's page at **www.amazon.com/author/pharmibrahim**

And please don't forget to follow me when you visit my author's page. Simply click or tap

on **Follow** button located below the profile picture.

Index

Made in the USA
Las Vegas, NV
23 November 2022

60158402R00243